PRAISE FOR

The Flirtation Experiment

"As the world tilts, our marriages need fresh survival skills. This book might just be that survival skills manual—except it reads nothing like a manual. I couldn't put it down! Each story is involving; every invitation feels equal parts awkward and exciting. Phylicia & Lisa have given both young and old marriages a gift in these pages. At twenty years in, I'm taking notes."

—Sara Hagerty, bestselling author, *Unseen: The Gift of Being Hidden in a World That Loves to be Noticed* and *Adore*

"If you find that your marriage is a little less magical and a little more mundane, *The Flirtation Experiment* might be just what the Love Doctor ordered. Filled with solid biblical truths, relevant real-life stories, and doable challenges and activities, this helpful resource will help spark your creativity and rekindle the romance you once felt toward your husband. I know I will be gifting it to many friends—whether they've been married for decades or for just a few days. Highly recommended."

—Karen Ehman, *New York Times* bestselling author, *Keep Showing Up: How to Stay Crazy in Love When Your Love Drives You Crazy*; speaker, Proverbs 31 Ministries; wife; and mom of five

"Could your marriage use a little more playfulness? Passion? Kindness? Hope? All of these things—and more—can be intentionally kindled, and in *The Flirtation Experiment*, Lisa Jacobson and Phylicia Masonheimer invite us into the laboratory of their lives to show us how it's done. Whether you've been married for five years or fifty, you'll find yourself challenged, inspired, and equipped to act the way you want to feel—and start enjoying the rich and satisfying relationship you've always wanted!"

—Jodie Berndt, bestselling author, *Praying the Scriptures for Your Life*

"You might ask me, 'So how did you like being a lab rat?' As it turns out, it was awesome! Lisa's experiment to find fun and frisky ways to engage with me pretty much guaranteed that. And this fun, light, and surprisingly deep book is the result. I love how Lisa and Phylicia take something so simple as encouraging wives to initiate flirting with their husbands and, from that unexpectedly profound opening, take them on a journey deep into a pursuit that leads to a holy place. Are you looking for new ways to keep your love alive and fresh? Don't miss out . . . keep reading!"

—Matt Jacobson, author, *100 Ways to Love Your Wife*, and at FaithfulMan.com

"After reading *The Flirtation Experiment*, I was both impressed and inspired by the effort and creativity Phylicia and Lisa put into bringing Matt and me back to the days when we dated our spouses. Truly a moving book!"

—Josh Masonheimer, husband to Phylicia and father of three, as featured in *The Flirtation Experiment*

"If you have been quietly hoping for change in your marriage, coasting along, or waiting for an easier season, *The Flirtation Experiment* is the kick start you need. This book is filled with practical help laced with gospel truth delivered by women who are living it out. It is the wit and wisdom we all need to infuse both fun and faithfulness back into one of the most important relationships of our lives. If you are ready to wisely tend to your marriage and have some fun doing it, this book will not disappoint."

—Katie Westenberg, author, *I Choose Brave: Embracing Holy Courage and Understanding Godly Fear*

"No matter how many years you've been married, you need this book! Our marriages are either growing or slowly dying; they won't remain status quo. We have to initiate growth. With unusual honesty, rich insights, and splashes of humor, Lisa and Phylicia give us ideas that will help us put a spark into our marriages."

—Susan Alexander Yates, speaker and author, *Cousin Camp: A Grandparent's Guide to Creating Fun, Faith, and Memories That Last*

"*The Flirtation Experiment* is loaded with simple even-you-can-do-it ideas for creating new energy in your marriage. Each chapter gives an illustration, biblical grounding, and encouragement for wives who want to take small steps that can have a big impact. I've been married more than thirty years and still came away with some fantastic ideas to use in my own marriage."

—Chris Taylor, *Honeycomb & Spice* and podcast cohost, *Sex Chat for Christian Wives*

"I often ask, 'How can you grow a better marriage if you do not know what the end goal looks like?' *The Flirtation Experiment* beautifully and authentically paints a picture of how to attain the goal of a connected, lighthearted, and harmonious marriage. Phylicia and Lisa balance candid anecdotes with theoretical insight and practical applications. I will be recommending this book to everyone in a healthy marriage because no matter what, there is always room for growth."

—Bonny Logsdon Burns, podcast cohost, *Sex Chat for Christian Wives*, and Betrayal Trauma Recovery Coach, StrongWives.com.

"Having had the chance to observe and hear about some of these experiments as they were happening, we were so excited to get our hands on this book! *The Flirtation Experiment* is full of eminently practical ideas expressed in sometimes raw, often funny, and always relatable stories from Phylicia's and Lisa's very different seasons of life as they share insecurities, victories, and, yes, theology, to inspire you to fan the flames of your marriage in approachable, achievable, countercultural ways."

—Josh and Chels Rief, CatzintheKitchen.com

"Refreshingly honest and packed with practical tips, *The Flirtation Experiment* is a permission slip to rediscover romance in the humdrum of married life. Phylicia and Lisa are gracious guides, ushering readers through their own experiences while constantly highlighting biblical truth. A delightful read for anyone looking to stop hitting the snooze button on their marriage."

—Ashlee Gadd, founder, Coffee + Crumbs, and author, *The Magic of Motherhood*

The Flirtation Experiment

the Flirtation Experiment

PUTTING MAGIC, MYSTERY, AND SPARK INTO YOUR EVERYDAY MARRIAGE

LISA JACOBSON AND
PHYLICIA MASONHEIMER

W Publishing Group
An Imprint of Thomas Nelson

Published in Nashville, Tennessee, by W Publishing Group, an imprint of Thomas Nelson.

The authors are represented by Alive Literary Agency, www.aliveliterary.com.

Thomas Nelson titles may be purchased in bulk for educational, business, fundraising, or sales promotional use. For information, please email SpecialMarkets@ThomasNelson.com.

Italics used in Bible quotations are the authors' own emphasis.

Library of Congress Cataloging-in-Publication Data

Names: Jacobson, Lisa, author. | Masonheimer, Phylicia, author.
Title: The flirtation experiment : putting magic, mystery, and spark into your everyday marriage / Lisa Jacobson, Phylicia Masonheimer.
Description: Nashville : W Publishing Group, 2021. | Includes bibliographical references.
Identifiers: LCCN 2021019309 (print) | LCCN 2021019310 (ebook) | ISBN 9780785246886 (hardback) | ISBN 9780785246893 (ebook)
Subjects: LCSH: Marriage—Psychological aspects. | Man-woman relationships—Psychological aspects. | Flirting. | Man-woman relationships—Religious aspects—Christianity. | Marriage—Religious aspects—Christianity. | BISAC: RELIGION / Christian Living / Love & Marriage | SELF-HELP / Personal Growth / Happiness
Classification: LCC HQ734 .J3263 2021 (print) | LCC HQ734 (ebook) | DDC 306.81—dc23
LC record available at https://lccn.loc.gov/2021019309
LC ebook record available at https://lccn.loc.gov/2021019310

Printed in the United States of America

21 22 23 24 25 LSC 10 9 8 7 6 5 4 3 2 1

Contents

Preface

PHYLICIA

Funny that it all began with a Hallmark movie.

It was a little before our fifth anniversary, at the height of those Hallmark Christmas movie marathons. My husband, Josh, was working long hours as an operations manager for a commercial restoration company; I was working from home during the day and watching our two little girls, ages four and two. This particular night he was away at a hockey game while I sat on the couch, a pint of mint chip ice cream as my companion.

I'm not the kind of woman who bases her life on Hallmark movies—I prefer the power of true stories to predictable romances. I don't read romance novels, and chick flicks are an every-once-in-a-while relaxation for me. But this particular night, something in this cheesy movie grabbed my attention.

The love story played out, and I noticed the tension, the playfulness, the suspenseful "does he like me?" feelings I remembered from my own dating days. Then, of course, there was the surprise kiss, the coy conversation, and the flirtatious look across the room that only he was meant to see. I stopped paying attention to the plot, wondering, *Why do so many of these things end when people get married?*

My marriage was not in crisis. We, like many young couples, were just busy with work, kids, and social commitments. Even with our monthly dates, marriage counseling, and dance lessons, neither of us felt truly fulfilled. Our daily interaction looked more like a meeting between coworkers than two lovers in the kitchen. I wanted the romance. I missed the mystery and fun of flirting with my boyfriend—and I was determined to put passion back in our relationship, as far as I was able.

I'm not alone in desiring a more romantic marriage. Fifty-nine percent of romance novel readers are coupled, aged thirty to fifty-four.[1] This begs the question, why are women in relationships seeking a romantic high from something *outside* their relationship? Probably because there's not much going on *inside* it.

Now, there are certainly two people in every marriage, both with the responsibility to pursue the other. Cultivating romance doesn't let husbands off the hook. What I recognized was this: I couldn't change Josh or make him more romantic, but I could take steps to be more romantic myself. I could set an example of pursuit. This required some reframing of pursuit in my mind.

In conservative Christianity, two words come with loads of baggage: *pursuit* and *flirtation*. Particularly for those acquainted with purity culture, these words contain a plethora of assumptions and expectations.

The assumption among some believers is that pursuit is a man's job. The complementarian belief is that the man—or rather, husband—is the spiritual leader. Some teachers expand this biblical ethic to include traditional cultural norms, arguing that because men are leaders, only men can show romantic interest. Only the man can ask a woman out, not vice versa. Only men initiate sex in marriage, and so on. But is this really what we see in Scripture? Are the distinct roles of men and women so limiting that women cannot even express romantic desire or passion for the men in their lives? Song of Solomon indicates otherwise:

> I am my beloved's, and his desire is toward me.
>
> *Come, my beloved, let us go forth* into the field; let us lodge in the villages.
>
> Let us get up early to the vineyards; let us see if the vine flourish, whether the tender grape appear, and the pomegranates bud forth: there will I give thee my loves.
>
> The mandrakes give a smell, and at our gates are all manner of pleasant fruits, new and old, *which I have laid up for thee*, O my beloved.
>
> —7:10–13 KJV

The wife in Song of Solomon even dreamed of pursuing her lover:

> On my bed by night
> *I sought him* whom my soul loves;
> *I sought him*, but found him not.
> I will rise now and go about the city,
> in the streets and in the squares;
> *I will seek him* whom my soul loves.
> *I sought him*, but found him not.
> The watchmen found me
> as they went about in the city.
> "Have you seen him whom my soul loves?"
>
> —3:1–3

In the New Testament, Paul indicated the mutual nature of desire (in this case, sexual) by commanding *both* husbands and wives not to deny each other without mutual consent (1 Cor. 7:5). Expanding beyond erotic love, we can look at 1 Corinthians 13 for a foundation of biblical love. This famous passage, so often quoted at weddings, tells us that love is patient and kind, not envious or rude. Love perseveres. It bears all things. In other words, loving other people is intentional. It's not an attitude of passivity, sitting on one's hands, waiting to respond. It's active. And these commands to love apply to both men and women—particularly to those married to each other.

Active love looks many ways. The 1 Corinthians 13 list is a great foundation. In marriage this love gets to be even more specific and—dare I say—spicy! There is mystery in the chemistry of man and woman, something Solomon himself observed:

> There are four things that are too mysterious for me to understand:
>
> an eagle flying in the sky,
> a snake moving on a rock,
> a ship finding its way over the sea,
> and a man and a woman falling in love.
>
> —Proverbs 30:18–19 GNT

Love is a choice and an action, but what about that initial infatuation? It plays a part as well. Combining the intentionality of biblical love with the passion and mystery of *falling* in love is powerful.

And then there is *flirtation*. In my conservative teen years, this was a cardinal sin. Girls wondered whether flirtation was okay, what it looked like, and whether or not their friends' actions toward boys qualified as flirting or just friendliness. Flirtation—I was taught—is inherently deceitful and insincere. But is that true?

Once I started dating, these regulations on flirtation became a heavy burden to bear. I debated whether I could show interest, and if so, how much? Where was the line for a godly woman who just plain *liked* a guy? As I dug deeper into the Word, I couldn't find a solid case against flirtation when it was expressed to a person you genuinely wanted to date. There was nothing dishonest or unladylike about expressing interest in a man. And as I raked through history on relationships and dating, I discovered that a woman's initiation was more accepted and normal than courtship culture would have me believe.

Scripture is actually very open to the idea of female pursuit in marriage. Since love reciprocates and initiates, it makes perfect sense for a wife to cultivate the chemistry she wants to see in her marriage.

So I got busy! I made a list of thirty ways I could flirt with my husband, ways I could pursue him intentionally. I took ideas from the Hallmark movie, but I also combed blog posts and articles from both secular and Christian sources. I read psychological journals on attraction and sexuality. What actions and attitudes encourage that "spark" in young relationships? That's what I wanted to know—and that's what I wrote down. Thirty items in hand, I started right away. I called it the Flirtation Experiment.

The first few days were hard. I was completely out of my comfort zone. I was nervous about appearing silly or out of character and was concerned that Josh would be puzzled by my behavior. And who could blame him? The Experiment required me to say and do things

I wouldn't typically do, but the only way to inject romance was to go all in. The first day, I sidled up to him at the kitchen sink and snaked an arm around his shoulders. "Your muscles are so strong you could probably lift the Empire State Building," I said sensuously (throwing up in my mouth as I did).

He was surprised. Then he laughed. He made a coy joke in return and kissed me as he left for work. I sighed in relief—it was over. I almost failed to notice his response.

The next day, the "kiss before work" was longer than normal. Rather than our usual peck, I pulled him in for longer. On day three, I was still uncomfortable and nervous—so I gave myself a little break by sending something via text. I made him a personalized playlist of songs and played it during dinner.

The first week of experiments was all like this—tiny changes in words, body language, and attention that took a little effort (and discomfort) on my part at the beginning. But on day seven, I noted on my phone:

> Noticed *his* attitude has changed. He brought me wine as a surprise. He takes an interest in my work. He asks about my day. Possibly because he knows he will get a playful response?

The next day, I wrote a further observation:

> Noticing that we tease as much as we used to, but the motive to the teasing has changed. It comes from a complimentary place, whereas it used to have a negative undertone . . . teasing about weaknesses or making fun of one another in front of others. Flirtatious

teasing always has a positive angle because you are appealing to the other person's emotions.

As the Experiment continued, it became easier and easier to implement. Trust was growing. I was feeling more fulfilled, and so was he. I wasn't the only one initiating romance; I was being romanced as well. The Flirtation Experiment was working!

Fascinated by what was happening in me and my marriage, I told my friend Lisa—married twenty-seven years compared to my five—what had occurred. She was intrigued, and we began talking about how this experiment could work for other women—women of all personalities, ages, and marriages. Would the steps I took work just as well for an introverted wife and extroverted husband like Lisa's relationship? Or for a couple who'd been married longer? Lisa shared that she had tried similar flirtatious experiments in her own marriage—and enjoyed similar results. Intentional pursuit looked a little different in her relationship and stage of life, but it still led to deeper intimacy and the romance we both craved.

Some of the things Lisa and I did with the Experiment aren't all that revolutionary. But *intention* and *consistency* made them powerful. Having the structure—and freedom—of a thirty-day experiment helped me feel as if I knew the next step, but I also wasn't trapped into something for more than one short month. I took the steps day by day, and day by day my marriage grew sweeter.

Intentional pursuit looked a little different in [Lisa's] relationship and stage of life, but it still led to deeper intimacy and the romance we both craved.

Lisa and I have a heart for thriving Christian marriages. We firmly believe that marriage is meant to make us holy—but holiness also includes joy. A godly marriage will also be a *happy marriage*—and it's okay for Christians to desire both. In 1 Timothy 6:6, Paul wrote that "godliness with contentment is great gain" (NKJV). Contentment is a heart attitude that does not strive for more than what it has. A contented marriage is a *happy* marriage, a marriage brimming with fulfillment. Godliness and happiness aren't at two ends of the biblical spectrum. They go hand in hand because we serve a God who is both righteousness and joy.

This experiment proved to satisfy our desire to pursue our husbands the way God intends—to live out a love that is creative and close, intimate, romantic, and everything those fictional books and movies promise is real. It's a way to put magic back into an otherwise everyday marriage and provides the structure to practice the powerful habits of affection, admiration, and affirmation.

Through these next thirty chapters, we give you some tangible examples of pursuit that you can use to bring holy happiness, mystery, and romance to your own marriage. We share what we did, how we felt about it, the barriers we had to overcome, and how our husbands responded to our flirtation. You can follow what we did, or you can create your own experiments inspired by each chapter's theme. We also discuss the biblical precedents for the flirtation experiments we chose to do.

Our hope is for your Flirtation Experiment to be more than a return to the excitement of your dating years; we pray it holds transformation for your heart and your husband's heart. May the power of pursuing love—and the fun of flirting with your man—be the beginning of something truly beautiful for you both.

Introduction

Before We Begin

PHYLICIA

Hello, sweet friend!

You've never had an invitation quite like this one! Lisa and I invite you to take a personal, real-time look at how we invest in our marriages. You won't find big promises on how to affair-proof your marriage or guarantees about learning to speak his language. In truth, we don't desire to tell you what to do at all, but we are genuinely excited to share with you what we did and what happened in our marriages.

Where, exactly, did the Flirtation Experiment lead? What started out as a desire to rekindle romance and closeness grew into something deeply profound and far more beautiful than we had anticipated. Not beautiful in the sense of everything turning out perfectly (which it never does!) but genuinely beautiful in how our loving God did a work in our hearts.

We're women who believe the Bible doesn't merely tolerate but actually encourages wives to embrace their desire for romance and the more luminous aspects of physical love. Longing for our husbands' romantic attention isn't only permitted in the Word; it's applauded by the One who created every starry night. Far from suppressing our true natures, the pages of the sacred text enliven a woman's desire to be desired by her husband.

Is This Book for You?

I've been married for seven years, Lisa for nearly thirty. We are at different stages of marriage and naturally have diverse pressures and priorities in many aspects of life. What does the Flirtation Experiment mean to a young couple or to one who is a little more seasoned?

Whether you're soon to be married, seven years in, or a veteran wife of decades, it doesn't matter. If you have a functional marriage but live with the sense that there may be a deeper, richer married life waiting for you, we are eager to share with you, and we sincerely hope this honest window into our marriages affirms in you God's best intentions for your own relationship. We also hope you will discover the freedom to be courageously proactive—empowered to act where you might have been less inclined or thought, *That's not what Christian wives are supposed to do.*

This book is for women interested in the full, biblical measure of their expression as women and as wives—unique creations of God—without the baggage and restraints of religion. It's for healthy Christian wives who thirst for more passion in their everyday relationships and could benefit from ideas on how to embark boldly on the journey.

We share our lives and experiences so that you, too, might find genuine empowerment and embrace your true liberty in the power of pursuit—enjoying the full measure of what God intended for your marriage. The Flirtation Experiment is a way to bring back magic, mystery, and excitement into our healthy but sometimes complacent marriages and—a bonus—to make the surprising discovery of a spiritual depth and substance that God intends in married love.

How to Customize the Experiment to Your Marriage

Josh and I have three children under the age of five. Matt and Lisa have eight children—their youngest, fifteen. We wrote this book together, representing two very different life stages. As you read through the experiments, you'll realize you don't have to do exactly what we did. Of course you can, but every marriage relationship is unique. Using the principles you find here, why not custom-design experiments of your own that fit your particular circumstances? And don't be bound by the format we followed. If you think your marriage needs it, why not spend a week—or even a month—on a specific theme?

What If He Doesn't Change?

Change can happen, but before you even start, you can choose not to be discouraged if it doesn't. The ideas in this book are a springboard, not a silver bullet to make everything perfect. Every husband is a different personality. Every marriage has its own story. Before you begin, remind yourself that the Flirtation Experiment is more about you than it is about changing your husband. He may not respond right away; you may need to seek counseling or biblical marriage coaching as the Experiment reveals areas of growth in your own hearts. There is no shame in seeking help to nurture your relationship's growth in strength and intimacy.

Very Important Who This Book Is *Not* For

The Flirtation Experiment is not intended as a fix for abusive, manipulative, sinful husbands, or as a tract of biblical proof texts as to why the Christian wife should persevere in a destructive relationship. We reject the idea that more sex, attention, serving, and dogged submission will change a sinful man who is abusing his wife. Are you struggling with a spouse who gaslights, manipulates, or otherwise seriously mistreats you? Are you in a situation that requires legal protection? Are you in a toxic, abusive relationship? Please don't look to this book as holding a possible answer. In fact, don't read this book at all. Seek professional, wise, biblical help and protection.

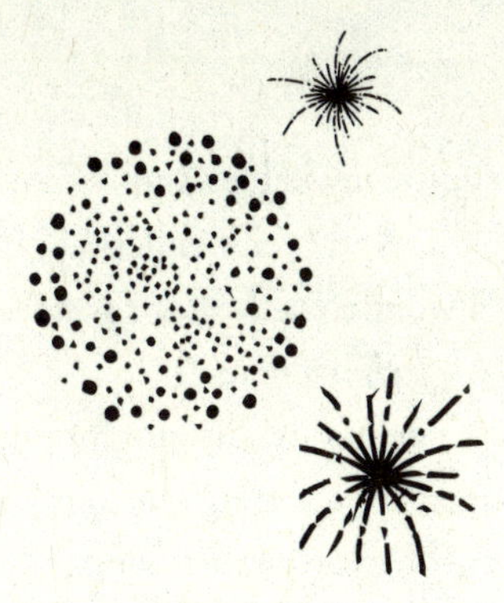

Chapter 1

Affection

PHYLICIA

The first time I took Gary Chapman's *The Five Love Languages* test, I got a zero for physical touch. *A zero.* Nowhere inside of me was there a desire to hug or be hugged, to touch or be touched; doing so made me extremely uncomfortable. As friends approached for a hug of greeting, I'd stiffly bend to meet them, wishing we could settle for a handshake. Is it any wonder my aversion to affection plagued my marriage?

I had no problem in the bedroom; it was almost as if I'd compartmentalized our physical interaction, placing any physical contact in the "sexual" part of my mind. As Josh left for work, I gave him the usual quick peck and returned to my busy day. Anything more than that? Not on my radar, and honestly I didn't want it to be.

As time passed and babies were born, any need for physical touch I might have had was consumed by holding, carrying, and feeding small children. I loved to cuddle my babies, but with my husband, there was a wall. He felt it. I felt it. And I felt helpless about what to do about it. *Is this just who I am?* I wondered. *I know I'm not expressing love the way he best receives it, but it feels too hard.*

I didn't realize it then, but my disdain for physical touch was actually fear. I was terrified that reaching out to my husband would result in rejection. This fear of rejection was so paralyzing, it was easier to pull back, to compartmentalize, than to express love physically.

Once I recognized what fear was doing to me and my marriage, I had a starting point. I couldn't change years of fear patterns overnight, but I could take small steps to fight back. My first step: touch Josh—not in a seductive or sexual way, but in the simple way one does to say, "I'm here, and I love you," instead of passing him like a coworker at the water cooler.

I tried it on one of those average Tuesdays, the kind full of dishes, laundry, and emails. When he was sitting at breakfast, I put my hands on his shoulders as we talked. When we discussed business plans in the afternoon, I came close to him instead of facing off like a player on an opposing team (my norm!). When we sat on the couch at the end of the day, I laid a hand on his arm.

It was new at first. I felt awkward. I was still getting cuddles and hugs and toddler kisses from children all day long, still satisfied without constant touching. But I noticed that these little efforts at affection, with no strings attached, made *me* more attached.

Josh noticed it too. He didn't say anything, but he squeezed my hand when I gave it. He came up beside me as I tossed laundry in the dryer and touched my shoulder too. It was like affection was contagious.

My personality fought against the vulnerability, but my heart was grasping for that single straw of hope. In loving him, I felt loved. Maybe affection wasn't to be feared after all.

Risking Affection

If you've read *The Five Love Languages*, you know that physical touch—as an expression of love—is not about sex. Physical touch is precisely what it sounds like: a hand on the shoulder, sitting close on the couch, hugging in the kitchen, and kisses with no agenda. What seems like such an easy way to show love is intimidating to those struggling with fear of openness.

This fear of being open has a name: *avoidant attachment*. People who grow up in homes where a parent is distant, extremely independent, or critical can develop this behavior. This avoidance manifests itself through evading physical or emotional closeness, suppressing emotions, becoming extremely independent like their parent, and getting claustrophobic when a partner tries to be affectionate. Fear of openness—vulnerability—can point to avoidant attachment. (A licensed professional counselor is a good starting point for processing this.)

Affection is, by nature, vulnerable, opening us up to the reactions or rejection of the person we love. For people who struggle with avoidant attachment, expressing affection is a risk.

My own avoidance held me back for most of our young marriage. I couldn't get past my innate fear of being rejected, unwanted, or—pridefully—looking silly. But as I looked at the legacy built by years of avoiding affection, I saw nothing but loneliness and heartbreak. The risk of showing love was worth healing in my marriage.

C. S. Lewis famously said about vulnerability: "Lock it up safe in the casket. . . . [and] it will become unbreakable, impenetrable, irredeemable."[2] I saw those words come true in my very own heart. How hard, distant, and unbreakable I became! I was safe, but I was not happy. And Josh? He was as lonely as I was.

In a Christian marriage, our model for love is Christ Himself.

Christ took on the most vulnerable, risky position in the world. He opened His heart to be broken by imperfect people and died to reconcile them to God. We are gathered into the arms of our Father, able to call Him the intimate name *Abba* (Rom. 8:15) because Jesus risked affection.

The *Affection* Experiment

Those first couple of times expressing affectionate touch felt completely antithetical to my personality. This made me nervous because I didn't want to feel like I was faking something. I wanted my actions to be genuine. But in the back of my mind was an adage from author Gretchen Rubin: "Act the way you want to feel."[3] In healthy situations, taking action can make our feelings catch up. For me, this was the case. As I reached out to Josh to show him love through physical touch, I felt more confident and at ease. I also felt closer to him. As for Josh, he was as surprised as I expected him to be. He knew how I struggled with showing my love physically, particularly as the one initiating. My reaching for him, tentative as it was, was received warmly. He pulled me closer when I reached out. He responded to my little touches with touches of his own. The first few times (and many times after), I was nervous. I knew he would be surprised at the change and questioned whether his reaction would feel like rejection to my fragile heart. But as I reminded myself of God's heart for my marriage—unity, passion, and love—I took the tiny step to embrace that truth.

The crazy part? God's truth became my truth. I felt closer to Josh because of seemingly insignificant touches. Our physical closeness reassured my heart; he *wasn't* disinterested in me. He wasn't rejecting me. I felt more known, more loved, and safer. And by the way he looked at me—and how he eagerly came to me each morning—I know he felt the same!

It's important to note that as I practiced affection with Josh, I was also working through my inner fears with the Lord. No number of experiments could fix that fear apart from His inner healing of my spirit. I prayed for a heart that felt safe in our relationship, and through that security, I could express safety to Josh as well. It was a small step, a little move toward openness and vulnerability that didn't result in rejection. Instead, it resulted in unity.

JOSH

When Phy did this experiment, it was awkward at first. But I tested high in physical touch on the love language test and was naturally drawn to reciprocate her efforts. That familiar phrase "Sex begins in the kitchen" definitely applies to me. My want and desire for intimacy in the bedroom is birthed out of being wanted and desired outside of the bedroom. This experiment is just what my love language prescribes as at least one way to my heart, creating emotional intimacy leading up to bedtime.

Your Flirtation Experiment

Perhaps what holds you back from affection isn't fear but busyness. How can you make time to show affection to your husband? What specific action would express affectionate love most? The seven-second kiss? Nonsexual touching? Holding his hand?

If you think fear is playing a role in your ability to show love physically, spend some time in the Word studying what God says about fear. How does He deal with it? What does He promise to those who follow Him?

Then decide on a simple act of affection to do today (and tomorrow) that will express your love in physical ways.

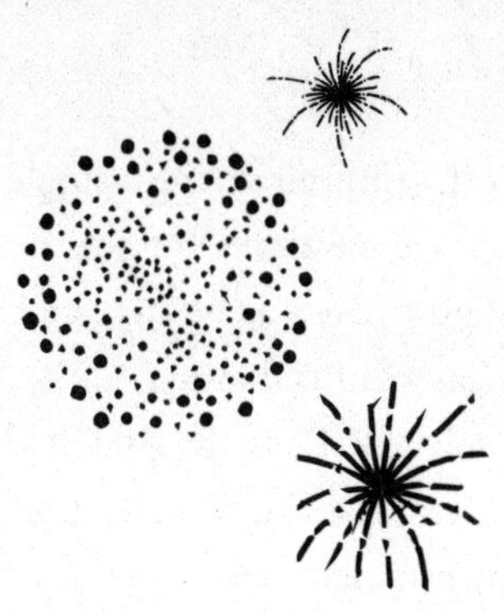

Chapter 2

Passion

LISA

I heard him walk through the front door, but I never even looked up. By the time my husband, Matt, came home that evening, I was so frustrated, so frazzled, that his coming home hardly mattered. I kept sautéing the onions and peppers without so much as a glance in his direction. I just ignored him and tried my best to tune out the squabbling of our four young kids hungrily sitting around the kitchen table.

I kept my eyes down, stirring those vegetables as if my life depended on it. And that's when I felt him come up behind me and slip his strong arms around my waist. I knew I should have felt cared for, but mostly what I felt was annoyed. Couldn't he see I was trying to make dinner? Couldn't he do something about the kids who were now throwing their napkins at one another across the table? Couldn't he do *something*?

I shrugged him off. Without saying a single word, I let him know that I wanted him to leave me alone. He got the message all right, and I saw his shoulders slightly drop as he stepped back. He stood silently behind me, watching as I sautéed away.

But then, out of nowhere, I had the wildest idea come into my head. What if . . . what if instead of brushing him off, I twirled around and leaned back into him? I suddenly had to know.

What if?

And then, right in that crazy kitchen moment, I turned off the stove, whipped around, and pressed my body deeply into his. And stayed there for a minute or more.

I don't know who was more surprised, him or me. He stared into my eyes, wondering what in the world had gotten into me. How could I explain it? That I was merely curious as to what might happen? That this was an impromptu experiment by an otherwise weary and worn-down mom of four?

How could I have known that one small move like this could start a much-needed, much-desired fire?

Igniting Passion

In all honesty, the last thing on my mind that evening as I stood over the skillet was passion. He wasn't expecting it, and I wasn't looking for it. We were in that survival stage of parenting when you find yourself in a bit of a blur as you go from one task to the next, trying to keep ahead of the cascading monotony of daily chores, milk spills, and utility bills.

Deep down he probably wished we had more sex, and I wistfully wanted more romance. But neither of us thought to ask the other as we were both doing what we could to keep up with the basic demands of the day until there was little left for the night. So we quietly kept our disappointments to ourselves and hoped something would change when our season changed.

Maybe that's where you find yourself—waiting for a new season. Hoping things will get better or hotter when there's more money, less stress, or better health, or when the kids are older. But here's what I'd say: Don't wait. Don't put passion on the back burner with some vague idea that it will reignite itself when your circumstances are different.

When I say "passion," I don't use it as some sort of euphemistic reference to sex (although sex typically plays a part in there somewhere). What I mean is that strong feeling of physical desire and closeness for each other—an intense longing.

Now, you may be asking yourself what place passion has in a Christian marriage. Isn't that a rather worldly, self-focused pursuit? A way of thinking better suited for chick flicks and romance novels? Something you leave behind not long after the honeymoon?

Don't put passion on the back burner with some vague idea that it will reignite itself when your circumstances are different.

God didn't leave passion to the world, and neither should we. The desire we have for our husbands is a beautiful part of how God designed us as women. To desire your man is to live in harmony with who you were created to be. Just think: God could have kept our marriage mechanical, but, instead, He gave us that extra spark. So, as believers, let's not be shy about seeking passionate Song of Solomon moments in our marriages. And we don't have to wait for our husbands to make the first move.

Lean into your man. Let the sparks fly!

Regretting having pushed away my husband's show of tenderness, I spontaneously decided to do the reverse. Rather than lean away from him, I spun around, wrapped my arms around him, and pressed into him even harder than he had embraced me.

What had come over me? Just minutes earlier, I'd felt resentful and ridiculously so. I was mad at him for coming home later than I'd wanted him to. It was the end of another hard day, and I felt overwhelmed by the many needs of our children, having been surrounded by them all day and yet feeling terribly alone at the same time.

Instead of rushing into my husband's arms as he walked through the door, letting him know how glad I was to have him home, I communicated the exact opposite—as if he was the last person I wanted to see right then, as if I'd be just as happy if he turned around and went back to the office. Having given my full attention to dinner prep and kid control, I had convinced myself that I legitimately had nothing left to give. Rather than warmly greeting the man I'd vowed to love, sizzling vegetables had become my priority. And, besides, I felt dull and unattractive standing there in my floral apron in front of the hissing pan. For most of us, that's about the furthest thing from feeling alive, warm, and sexy, isn't it?

For this spur-of-the-moment experiment, I had to overcome my self-pity, self-doubts, and self-focus (I know, that's a lot of "self," isn't it?) and turn my attention to what was best for us both, right then. And what began as an almost mechanical act—a forced decision more than a natural impulse—quickly grew into something magical.

Only a few seconds into it, and I was feeling the heat as much as he must have. But the surprising response didn't stop with that moment.

The effect on him was far greater, far broader than I could have anticipated. Maybe you're thinking, *No, wait, let me guess . . . he wanted to take you to bed after dinner and have sex.*

Yes, I think that's fairly safe to say! But the outcome was so much bigger than that. He felt close to me—wanted and welcomed and, well, *like a man*. He also became noticeably energized and ready to dive into what was needed in the situation. I went back to our dinner on the stove (with face flushed, I'll admit it!) while he entertained the kids until the meal was ready.

Strange to think that I had felt so drab—both undesiring and undesirable—that evening, having no idea how quickly things could heat up between us once I made a definitive choice. Right there in the middle of the kitchen on an ordinary weekday night, I started a small blaze.

MATT

> Men are microwaves, women slow cookers? Not in our house. We have two microwaves! I just love how Lisa chose to change in the moment and reached for me, because it said everything. We're not just married. We're friends and lovers. For me, that's living the dream.

Your Flirtation Experiment

Our embrace in the kitchen that night rekindled a passion for my husband that I'd pushed down so deep that it had nearly been forgotten. What is one small way you could heat things up in your marriage relationship? A sensual touch, an unexpected flirtatious squeeze, or a lingering kiss? Try it out and see if it doesn't set off some sparks!

Have you been waiting for your husband to make the first move? If that's you, take some time to read the Song of Solomon, and you'll find a fresh perspective on the topic. It's a relatively short book in the Bible, consisting of eight poetically written chapters, so it's possible to read one chapter a day (and two on Sunday) to read the entire book in a week. You might even want to take a few notes.

Or if you've been holding back because you're waiting until you feel the longing, try making your move first and then let the feelings follow. Consider the specific way you can make passion a greater priority in your marriage.

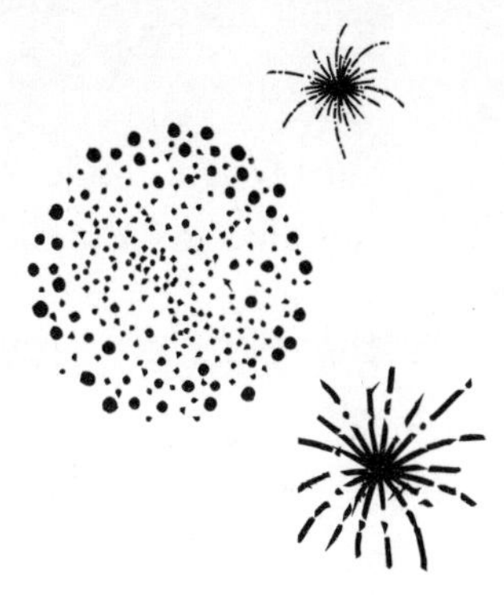

Chapter 3

Playfulness

PHYLICIA

I heard Josh rustling through grocery bags, putting flour and cans of fruit on the pantry shelf.

"Oh ho, what is this?!" he said, peering around the kitchen corner. He held up a pack of Little Debbie Fudge Rounds.

"Don't show the girls," I whispered. "Those are for us!"

He couldn't keep them off his mind. As soon as our toddler and kindergartner were in bed, he was hankering for the taste of childhood.

"I'll get some," I offered—because I had a plan.

I had googled a list of pranks the day before, fully intending to prank my husband. I opened the box (did you know these boxes open sideways?), dumped all the Fudge Rounds into the back of the pantry, and stuck two carrots of equal weight inside. Then I wrote, "hahahaha," on the cardboard and walked back to the living room.

Did I mention Josh hates carrots?

That wasn't my first trick, however. A few days before, Josh had asked for a cup of tea, which I obligingly went to get—returning with a mug full of paper *T*s. He found this prank so funny he took a picture for social media, a rare effort for my internet-averse husband.

Playfulness, like laughter, isn't something to which I'm naturally attuned. My bent toward the serious, the heavy, and the eternal can make me a little boring at times. Pranking Josh gave me some quick, easy ways to make him laugh.

But this was only the beginning of my learning how to play. A few days after my pranks, I was writing in my prayer journal, praying over my marriage and family. I closed the book and began to wash dishes. As I washed them, I sensed the Lord speaking to my heart, the voice I know better than any: *I want you to play video games with your husband.*

I almost dropped a plate. *Excuse me, Lord?* I'm used to conversing with the Lord throughout the day. I'm even accustomed to His specific leading in certain situations. But this? It was *so* specific, and—worst of all—*I hate video games.*

A source of great conflict in our early marriage, video games were the bane of my existence. Josh grew up playing them; I grew up despising them. As time went on, we came to an agreement that Josh would play video games only once or twice a week, usually when the girls were in bed. This seemed fair. "You do you, bro," was my attitude on the subject—although my distaste for the games had not lessened.

So to sense the Lord leading me not to just smile upon his hobby but to *participate in it* . . . not my cup of *T.*

Playfulness As Intimacy

Whenever the Lord leads me specifically, I ask a few questions: Does this line up with Scripture? Is this consistent with the character of God? How can I obey in this area?

Josh doesn't play violent or racy video games, so I knew the games themselves didn't contradict the standards of the Word. And investing in my marriage definitely *does* line up with both the Word and the character of God. The only thing left for me to answer was, how will I obey?

Answering that question takes a little look at playfulness as intimacy. Why do so many of us cease the playful part of flirting once we've said our vows? The feisty, fun, mysterious aspect of play in a relationship is part of how we fall in love. In a way, it's intimacy.

One reason we avoid play is because of the risk. Being playful exposes us. *What if he doesn't laugh? What if he doesn't reciprocate? What if he doesn't care?* Play requires risk, which is why so many of us don't pursue it. Marital therapist R. William Betcher put it this way: "Playing is a reconnoitering of the unknown borders of two psyches, whose contours can become reassuringly familiar only through the experience of mutual vulnerability and nonjudgmental responsiveness. It is through playing that we learn how to approach someone's more intimate self."[4]

Why do so many of us cease the playful part of flirting once we've said our vows? The feisty, fun, mysterious aspect of play in a relationship is part of how we fall in love.

While busyness, being in my own head, and my personality alter how I perceive playfulness, there's a deeper reason at play. Betcher points out that playful relationships require "vulnerability and nonjudgmental responsiveness." Vulnerability, judgment, and the risk of negative response just so happen to be my fear trifecta. I don't want to look stupid or feel embarrassed, so I don't risk being silly. I don't do things I'm not interested in. I refuse to play.

But in refusing to play, am I refusing intimacy too? Could doing something fun (or funny) bond us together? Just like laughter in Scripture, play—which often leads to laughter—can bring us together in a "bond of peace" (Eph. 4:3). In fact, verses 2–3 say, "Be completely humble and gentle; be patient, bearing with one another in love. Make every effort to keep the unity of the Spirit through the *bond of peace*" (NIV).

Maybe taking time to play with our spouse requires humility. Maybe it requires patience and bearing with each other's love for video games. Maybe, by playing with our husbands, we learn how to love.

The *Playfulness* Experiment

Only a day after I sensed the Lord calling me to play video games with Josh, he came into the kitchen carrying a plastic grocery bag. "I found something in the basement," he said. "I was thinking it might be fun for us to play it together."

"What is it?" I asked. The bag was lumpy and full of black cords.

"It's my GameCube. I have a game called *Mario Party* I think you might enjoy . . . or at least, dislike less." He walked off with the bag, and I was left with the sneaking suspicion that God had ganged up on me.

A few days went by, and Josh didn't mention the game again. I decided to bring it up.

"Do you want to play that game you mentioned?" I hinted, after the oldest two kids were in bed.

"It's kind of hard to set up. Maybe I can get to it tomorrow," he replied.

Ugh! I'm actually making an effort here, and he isn't even interested.

I tried again the next day. "I'm game to play that game. We could tonight?"

He looked at his calendar. "Sorry, I have hockey. Maybe we can do it later this week?"

Now I was quite perturbed. Who knew playing a game would take so much effort? It was starting to look like I wanted to play video games more than he did. A few days went by, and finally we found a night to give it a shot. At this point, I was genuinely curious about the game—I'd waited almost a week to play it. The baby finished his bottle, and we laid him down next to us to play.

"This is a team-style game; that way we work together, not against each other," Josh said.

We played for an hour, and by the end of it . . . *I liked the game*. It was fun. I can hardly believe I'm writing that, after having disavowed the games for so many years—but it was fun for me and clearly fun for him. There was a visible connection between my enjoyment and his. Our years together have not brought us many things we both enjoy, and we've often struggled with leisure activities because our interests are so different. But by thoughtfully entering his arena, those differences were set aside. I could tell that seeing me enjoy his hobby made him enjoy it even more.

Your Flirtation Experiment

Indulging in your spouse's hobbies can be really hard—a true challenge. But if you try it, what hobby would you choose? Or maybe being playful looks like pranking your husband (maybe start by going easier on him than Nair in the shampoo bottle!), telling jokes, or putting down your phone and intentionally, flirtatiously having a full conversation. Playfulness can look many ways.

I found it most helpful to think back to our dating days. What about me was appealing? I was up for anything—aside from video games, of course. I was sassy and funny and engaging, whether we were at the gym or at a mini-golf course.

Ask yourself, *What could I do to enter into my spouse's world for a day (or evening)? What will my playfulness experiment be?*

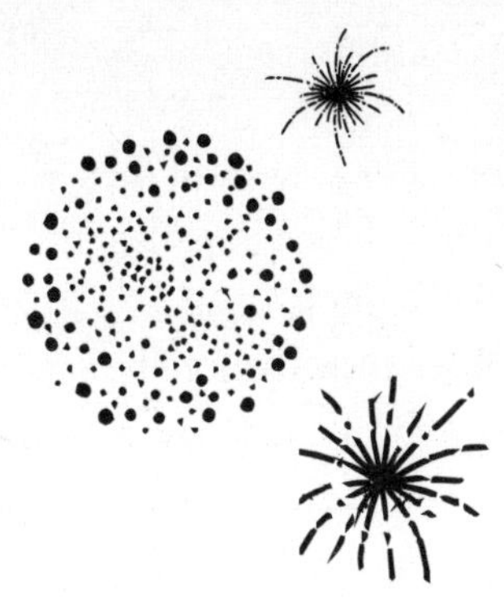

Chapter 4

Kindness

LISA

Odd to think that this experiment was inspired by a complete stranger. But it's a fact.

I left the house in such a rush, trying to get those last few errands in before our appointment later in the afternoon, only to find myself stuck in the slowest line at the grocery store. Wondering what the holdup could possibly be, I peered around the person in front of me to see what was taking so long.

And that's when I saw her. It took only a few seconds to realize this cashier was having a terrible day and seemed set on taking it out on the rest of us. She deliberately took her sweet time ringing up each item, then carelessly tossed it into the shopping bag. The expression on her face said it all: *Yeah, well, what are you gonna do about it?* I tried to think of my options, but as none of them sounded too Christian, I simply waited my turn with one impatient eye on the clock. After all, my day wasn't over. Far from it.

In the end, the delay turned out to be a mercy. The extra minutes of waiting in line gave me a chance to cool down, and when I got a little closer to her, I could see eyes of worry, fear, and pain. It wasn't that she was merely having a hard day. Life had been . . . was . . . hard. It's amazing how God can change our perspective.

Kindness, it suddenly occurred to me. *That's what this woman needs right now. Not impatience. Not frustration. She needs a gentle word of kindness.*

And so, by the time I got to the front of the line, I had a reasonably good grip on my attitude and greeted her warmly. She mumbled something about "everything going wrong," and I said I was sorry, sympathetically adding that it was okay; it happens to all of us.

Astonished, she looked up from the register and saw that I sincerely meant it. From there we struck up a pleasant conversation as she finished bagging my groceries. Her eyes appeared a bit brighter, and maybe it was only my imagination, but I thought she moved a little faster too. I'd like to think our exchange became a turning point for her day. It certainly had become one for mine.

Except my day didn't stop there.

When I finally arrived back home on this unusually stressful day, I received a phone call from Matt, telling me he was running late. Things at work didn't go as expected, and so he was going to miss our long-planned appointment. Now we'd have to cancel and reschedule for another day.

I nearly dropped the phone. *How in the world could he do this to me?* Instantly furious, I felt heat race up my neck and into my face. Here I had run around all that afternoon like a madwoman to make it home in time for our appointment, only to have it turn out to be for nothing. This was the last straw, and I could feel myself snapping.

Maybe nothing could be done now, but I wanted to make sure he understood how much he'd messed up my plans. I wanted him to feel as bad as I did. Maybe even worse.

But just as I was ready to lash out, a word from earlier in the day suddenly confronted me: *kindness.*

I was instantly reminded of when I said no to my first impulse and chose kindness for *a total stranger at the grocery store.* For her, I had decided to show love, kindness, and patience. Not because she particularly deserved it (you could argue the opposite), but because it was the loving, Christlike thing to do.

But, for the man I'd married? *Daggers!*

Now, why should it be any different for him?

Oh, conviction.

"Babe, are you still there?"

I'd remained speechless for so long that Matt asked if I was still on the line. I took a deep breath and responded with something soft, understanding, and right—rather than the clipped, resentful remarks previously sitting on the tip of my tongue.

I surprised him with kindness.

In my head, I could hear someone saying, "Oh, I'm sorry it's been such a crazy day. No worries, we can always reschedule. I'll see you when you get home, babe." Certainly it was my voice, but I was nearly as startled as he must have been. What I was saying, and, more importantly, *how* I was saying it, was rather different from my initial response.

Surprise Him with Kindness

Don't you find it interesting—if not downright convicting—that we can find it in our hearts to demonstrate Christian kindness to our friends, our neighbors, or even a total stranger yet struggle to offer that same compassion to our own husbands?

Don't you find it interesting—if not downright convicting—that we can find it in our hearts to demonstrate Christian kindness to our friends, our neighbors, or even a total stranger yet struggle to offer that same compassion to our own husbands?

Maybe we think, *Oh, he can take it*, or *I just have to be myself.* Or maybe we justify it with *It's not like I can be perfect.* I get it. I've had all those same thoughts.

But what about those Bible verses, such as Ephesians 4:32, that instruct us to be kind to one another? And Colossians 3:12, which tells us that as God's chosen ones, we are to put on kindness? Surely those passages are intended not only for the people "out there" but also for the people nearest us, beginning with the ones by our sides.

Ask the Lord to help you be kind to your husband—with the words you speak, the tone you use, and the actions you take.

Go ahead, surprise him with your kindness today. Because love is kind.

The *Kindness* Experiment

Choosing kindness was more challenging than I expected but also more rewarding than I anticipated. Although I like to think of myself as a kind person, I realized that I can be kind when I *feel* like it—and especially when it's toward my husband. When I'm upset or frustrated, I feel the freedom to snap at him whether he is the cause or not. Somewhere I got this idea that if someone loves you, then you should be honest with them, and they should be able to take it.

But then came the sudden moment of conviction that my response doesn't fit the definition of love found in the Bible—1 Corinthians 13:4, for instance: "Love is patient and *kind*." What's worse, how awful to realize that I found it easier to show kindness to a grumpy cashier at the grocery store than to my own husband. *Ouch*.

Now, why is that? This is where I had to take a good, long look at myself. My first inclination was to make him pay for what I perceived as messing up my day. Second, I was afraid that if I let him get away with it, then it would reduce his motivation to improve. I reasoned that if I punished him for disappointing me, then he'd try harder the next time.

I can't say I was conscious of any of these thoughts at the time. My natural impulse was to lash out, and it was my earlier experience in the grocery store that stopped me from carrying it out. Even though it sounded almost strange, not quite honest in the moment, I felt better after we hung up the phone. My husband never said anything about my atypical response to that call, but I thought I heard relief in his voice when we said our goodbyes. And by the time he returned home, we were both ready to redeem what was left of our evening together.

Your Flirtation Experiment

Maybe this aspect of the Experiment sounds more like a test than an experiment to you. Either way, I think you'll be pleased by the effect your kindness can have on both you *and* your husband.

Start by taking a few minutes to identify those situations where you might struggle to show kindness to your husband. In my case, it would be when he comes home late or misses our engagements, but it might be something else in your relationship. Whatever it is, decide ahead of time that you're going to respond with unexpected, and possibly undeserved, kindness. Keep reminding yourself: *love is kind, love is kind, love is kind.*

My kindness experiment focused on choosing what my reaction or response would be in what felt like an exasperating situation. But you might also consider the many ways you can initiate kindness toward your husband: a kind word, a kind action, or even choosing to have kind *thoughts* toward him.

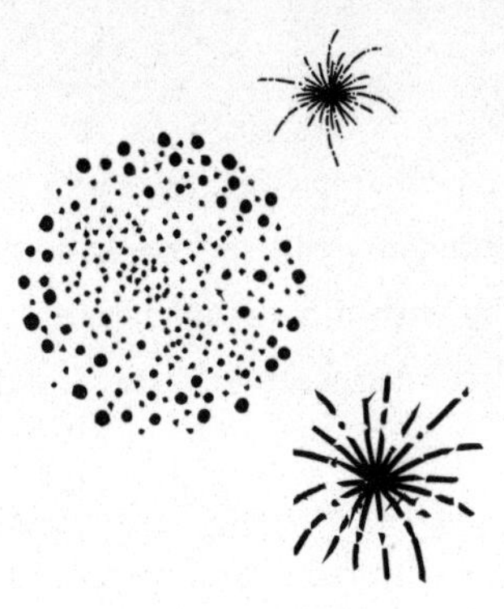

Chapter 5

Desire

PHYLICIA

I put the baby in his crib and watched him drift off to sleep. *Do I go to bed now, or do I stay awake?* I mused. He was waking at least once, sometimes as many as four times, a night. It was a crapshoot which it would be, and I wanted to get as much sleep as I could.

But I also knew . . . it had been almost two weeks. Two weeks since *you know what.*

I was annoyed at the decision. Annoyed that I didn't really want to have sex. Annoyed that my desire wasn't there. Annoyed at my squishy postpartum body. Not so long ago I was the one with a higher drive, and now here I was, trying to invent reasons to go to sleep at 8:00 p.m. What had happened?

That was a rhetorical question, because I knew full well what had happened. Life. Kids. Work. Changes. I knew the ups and downs of desire were normal, probably hormonal and definitely due to tiredness too. But I wanted my old self back! I wanted Josh to know I really *did* enjoy being with him—but the time was never right. When offered the choice between sleep and sex, the new me almost always chose sleep.

There was a time in our marriage when this scenario was completely reversed. I was the one with the higher drive, and I felt the sting of rejection. Josh was in a stressful season of work, and my initiation wasn't always welcomed. I knew all too well how it felt to be turned down, how personal the sting, even if that wasn't the intention. Josh never complained when I was tired, but I wanted better for us (as our season allowed). I wanted some of the spark and mystery back in the bedroom. But how—with three kids and so many responsibilities and a body that wasn't like I wanted it—could I make it happen?

Hollywood Sex

Before marriage, I assumed couples had sex every night. I thought, if you can do it, why not?! I had an idea about sex formed by movies and media that wasn't realistic to the everyday experience, or at the very least not sustainable for years to come. I had no concept of the ups and downs of life together and how that can alter desire through the years. Hollywood sex promised constant craving any time and every time a couple got together.

Other voices told me that sex would end when we had kids. Dire statements like, "You'll never sleep again"; "You won't even want it"; and "Who has time for that?" painted a depressing picture of parenthood. Add to that the negative and unbiblical teachings about sex in the church—"You need to have sex, or your husband will stray"; "If he asks, you must *always* say yes"; "It's a wife's duty to her husband"—and it's no wonder many wives are confused, guilty, and burdened by the very idea of intimacy.

In truth, these narratives play off one another. If you believe sex will always meet the glamorized Hollywood standard, then, yes, having kids will be a difficult transition. If you believe the twisted teachings from an off-base church, sex will become dutiful and even painful. Worse, it can even become a cover for manipulation and abuse. But what if desire—in a healthy marriage—is so much more than what these sources sell us?

In Proverbs 5, the older and wiser author told a younger man to rejoice in the love of his wife:

> May your fountain be blessed,
> and may you rejoice in the wife of your youth.
> A loving doe, a graceful deer—
> may her breasts satisfy you always,
> may you ever be intoxicated with her love.
>
> —VV. 18–19 NIV

Okay, Solomon, you're getting a little PG-13 here! I think it's fair to say this verse applies just as much to wives as to husbands. After all, the author of Proverbs also wrote Song of Solomon—a beautiful depiction of *mutual* desire. It is not wrong to "rejoice" in your husband. It is not wrong to want to be satisfied by him and to be completely overwhelmed by his love. Nor is it wrong to tell him you're tired (1 Corinthians 7 emphasizes the mutual nature of desire). Sexual desire is important, but equally important is a simple desire for your spouse *himself*. I would argue that this is a foundational element of a good sex life. When we are desired holistically, loved for who we are and what we bring to the relationship, sexual desire has room to grow. That goes for women, but it also applies to men.

As with most things romantic, my tendency (and maybe yours) is to put things like desire and flirtation at the very end of my to-do list. They're there if I get to them. Surprise—I rarely do! To really rejoice in my husband, I have to move desire further up, toward the top of my list. But how could desiring Josh be more important than unloading the dishwasher? Getting the girls' homeschool done? Sending that marketing email? Can't it wait?

***Sexual desire is important, but equally important is a simple desire for your spouse* himself.**

Yes, it can. But in my marriage, that waiting wore on day after day, until I never had time to desire Josh at all. I didn't think about it except for the every-ten-days when he initiated something in the bedroom. In hormonal seasons, such as postpartum, I give myself grace—and so does he. But at the same time, I know our marriage feels more connected, more fun, and fierier when I "rejoice in the husband of my youth."

The *Desire* Experiment

I could have made this experiment about having sex. And full disclosure: that's how it ended! But I knew that the real issue regarding desire was more complicated than that. Josh needed to know I desired him as a person, to be with him in general, not just in the bedroom. He needed to know I liked him, not just loved him, and that I liked him for who he was—not just what he could do for me. My previous experiment with affection and playfulness laid the groundwork for this one.

We usually sit in matching armchairs to watch TV in the evenings. But I noticed that the coffee table between our chairs often blocked our view of each other, and we definitely couldn't sit together while watching. So, the day before this experiment, I rearranged the living room so the couch faced the TV instead. For Josh, whose love language is physical touch, I knew this would send the message that I liked to be close to him. Our armchairs are comfy and convenient, but the closeness makes a difference for him.

I made a cheese plate and served it with our favorite bottle of wine. I picked out a show we both love and lit my fireplace display of candles.

"What's the occasion?" Josh asked, slightly confused.

"None, I just wanted to be with you."

I snuggled up to him on the couch, my phone turned off in another room. He put one arm around my shoulders and with his other hand scooped some of the brie. I gave him my full attention, saying with eyes and words and body: *I desire you for who you are.* It wasn't much, but it was my effort to say, "I am my beloved's, and his desire is for me" (Song 7:10).

Your Flirtation Experiment

In a healthy marriage that simply needs a little spark, the desire experiment can be a fun surprise. If initiating sex (for your sake, not just his) and being explicit in your desire is new to you, chances are it will be new to your husband too. Sometimes stepping into our desire and confidence as sexy, pursuing wives feels intimidating. Don't think this requires becoming someone you're not. Show your desire in a way that fits who you are—the woman your husband fell in love with.

For me, pretty nightgowns, lounge sets, and lingerie help me feel more myself. I love the elaborate, sweet-smelling, and beautiful. It might be different for you. Maybe setting up a fancy home date is your thing, or arranging a dinner out, complete with heels and lipstick, and even more longing upon the return home. Think about what you admire about your husband and what made you desire him when you first met. Let that inspire your experiment!

As you consider your own experiment, I want to make an important caveat: sex is not a solution for abusive or manipulative marriages. If your husband uses sex to manipulate, guilt, or intimidate you, please seek counseling and outside help.

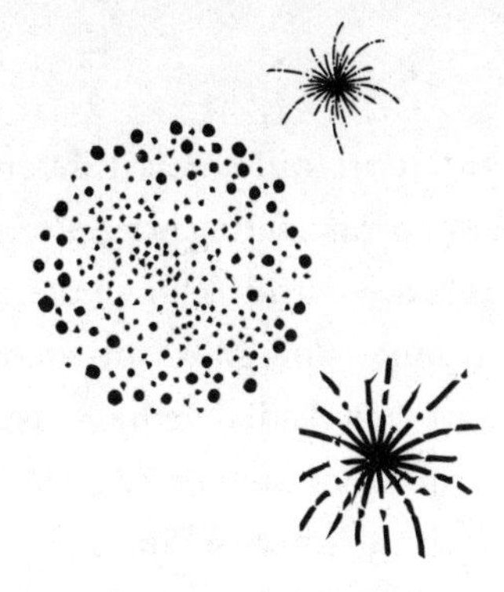

Chapter 6

Adventure

LISA

Matt finished his phone call and said nothing for some time, but his active eyes were chasing some thought around his head. After a while, I couldn't contain my curiosity and asked, "Where have you gone?"

"Exploring," he answered. "My friend just reminded me of how much I used to enjoy exploring—how I would take off into the wilderness for hours, days, and even weeks. I've never seen a horizon I didn't desire to know what was on the other side."

Ah yes, the explorer and adventurer. That's my Matthew. Nothing too revelatory there.

Except, once we started raising our children and also caregiving for both of his parents, those things put a bit of a damper on the adventurous life. Sure, Matt still enjoyed dreaming, studying, and watching documentaries of fascinating places and ancient architecture, but that was hardly the same thrill as going there.

Without really meaning to, my grand adventurer had been grounded for more than a few years now. And something in me told me it was high time we changed that situation. But how? And where?

In my wildest dreams, I'd send him off to some faraway place where he could explore to his heart's content: Göbekli Tepe, Petra, and Machu Picchu are a few on his long list. In reality, however, we have neither the time nor the budget to do anything quite at that level. For the time being, I needed to settle for a local adventure experiment, one that I could realistically pull off and, preferably, one we could do together.

But I was stumped for ideas.

Life-Giving Adventure

I wish you could meet John and Susan—my favorite couple, married for more than fifty years. You would love them! Although we share a number of wonderful memories now, I'll never forget the first time we had breakfast together. The two of them had flown into town to speak for a marriage conference, and we met them at a nearby restaurant after they had finished their commitment.

There we were, enjoying a lovely time talking about all kinds of subjects, when the conversation turned to how they'd spend the rest of the day since they weren't due back home until the following morning.

"Oh, we're going snowmobiling up on Mount Bachelor!" Susan enthusiastically informed us.

Really? It was difficult to hide my astonishment. I just don't know that many seventy-year-olds who fly to Oregon and then snowmobile.

Trying to sound nonchalant, I said, "I didn't realize you two were snowmobilers. How fun!"

"But we're not. This will be our first time trying it," Susan cheerfully announced.

There was no hiding it now; I was shocked. "You're telling me that you've never been snowmobiling before, but now here you are heading up to Mount Bachelor to give it a try?"

Although I didn't add "*and in your seventies, no less!*" it was implied.

Susan laughed. (Susan always laughs.) "Yes! The way to keep young is to keep doing new things."

You can believe that right then and there I started taking notes. Not only do I have a deep admiration for my adventurous friends, but I am also greatly inspired by their marriage of fifty years. More than merely surviving those five decades together, they're one of the few couples I know who continue to thrive and enjoy each other after so many years. I was more than eager to learn any secrets they had to offer.

So we ordered another French press coffee, and the conversation continued. I gleaned many marvelous insights from our talk together, as well as others that would follow, but one thing resonated that day: I had a new appreciation for the value of adventure.

I'm not suggesting that snowmobiling in the Oregon Cascades or hiking in Aspen, Colorado (like John and Susan did this past summer), is the baseline standard, but there's certainly much to be said for stepping out and doing something that is totally "other" than your daily routine. And I have been on the lookout ever since for those things that might fit Matt and me in this season of fewer options that we find ourselves in.

The *Adventure* Experiment

On a recent cold winter afternoon, out of nowhere and in the middle of the week, I looked at Matt and said, "Let's go for a drive up into the Cascades."

"Right now?" he asked, understandably confused. "Who are you, and what have you done with my wife?"

I'm not exactly known for being spontaneous.

"Yep! Only you have to buy me a latte before we get too far down the road."

In a few short minutes he had keys in hand, and we were climbing into the car. As promised, he stopped by the coffee kiosk, and then we headed toward Three Creeks—driving a long way up the mountain, as far as we could until the tires started slipping too much on the ice (just the way Matt likes it).

And maybe we had been on this road before. But it was some time ago, and the day was so dramatically beautiful that it hardly mattered. We were on an adventure, and it felt thrilling—in a small-scale kind of way. Better yet, we both felt much closer after having shared our snowy mountain experience.

Your Flirtation Experiment

Maybe you have the resources to plan a big adventure, or perhaps you need to take a more modest approach. What would your husband enjoy? If you're a novice or maybe just very rusty when it comes to adventure, start with something simple so you'll have a good chance for success. Plan a short hike or explore a nearby nature reserve. Swim in the river or borrow bikes for the day. Rent a boat (and maybe a skipper too) or go on a fishing expedition.

My husband is the more adventurous one in our marriage, but you may be the adventurer in yours. If so, you'll want to think up something your man would be down for trying as well.

If you're a novice or maybe just very rusty when it comes to adventure, start with something simple so you'll have a good chance for success.

Some adventures, such as snorkeling, backpacking, skydiving, canoeing, cycling, rafting, and snowmobiling(!), require learning a new skill, so it might be wise to sign up for a class or lessons before you head out on your next expedition, which could be a fun adventure all in itself.

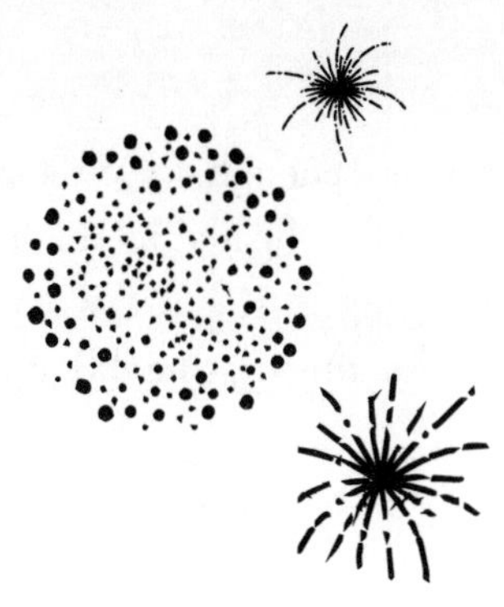

Chapter 7

Laughter

PHYLICIA

I am a nervous laugher.

If I'm in an uncomfortable social situation, my response of choice is to laugh. In my days of office parties and Junior League holiday gatherings, I'd find myself chortling at the dumbest of jokes just to make the joke teller feel better about himself—and to assuage my own discomfort.

It was a harmless habit until I got engaged and discovered how much can go wrong when you laugh at the wrong things. Josh and I spent a good deal of time with a particular couple during our engagement. The man in that couple was quite the jokester: you'd be in his presence less than ten minutes before the puns started flying.

But the puns alone were not enough; knee-slapping exuberance went with them, such that I felt obligated to laugh along. How could I just leave the joke hanging in the air? Worried I would hurt his feelings, I laughed just as much as he did at jokes I thought were half as funny.

After one double date, the ride back to my apartment was eerily quiet.

"What's wrong?" I asked Josh.

"Why do you think he's so funny?" Josh replied.

"I don't!" I exclaimed. "I'm laughing to be nice."

"I just don't understand why you laugh so much at what *he* says and hardly laugh at all when I make a joke," Josh said.

The car plunged into silence. I looked out the window, watching rain droplets chase each other into the dark. Why *did* I laugh at the silly jokes of a friend's husband but roll my eyes at my fiancé's?

The longer I thought about it, the truth became clear: I was afraid of making other people feel bad. But I also didn't want my own fiancé's puns to reflect on me. I was willing to laugh with an acquaintance because he wasn't linked to me, willing to do my social duty of making him feel welcome (bad jokes and all). But when it came to Josh, laughing was off the table.

I didn't laugh because I was proud.

Years have helped me destroy that double standard, but I still find myself too proud, too busy, too "mannerly" for laughter. My desire to be respected can cause me to downplay and ignore opportunities to laugh. I came to marriage with no interest in silliness, and I'm married to a man who *loves* a good dad joke. What happened in our engagement shed light on how much Josh enjoys when I laugh with him, get a chuckle at one of his painful puns, and generally join him in . . . joy.

The God Who Laughs

Because Christians know God is holy, we emphasize the need for holiness in our lives. Holiness is essential to our communion with God and was bought for us at the highest cost—the life of Christ. But in pursuit of holiness, we sometimes veer off course, pretending that joy and holiness are on two ends of a spectrum. To be happy, to laugh, is less spiritual than to do hard and holy things. This could not be further from the truth.

Scripture portrays a God whose holiness and joy are intertwined. They are so grown into each other that to be holy is to be happy, and joy itself is a fruit of the Spirit (Gal. 5:22–23). Psalm 16:11 says, "You make known to me the path of life; in your presence there is fullness of joy; at your right hand are pleasures forevermore."

The fullness of joy is found in God's presence. Not just that—all things good and pleasurable are found with Him too. God's holiness is not the absence of fun and laughter. His holiness frees us to be fully alive.

To be holy is to be happy, and joy itself is a fruit of the Spirit.

In John 15:11 Jesus told His disciples the "why" behind His teachings. "These things I have spoken to you," He said, "that my joy may be in you, and that your joy may be full." Everything Jesus taught regarding God, man, and morality was to bring His people *fullness of joy*. His sacrifice, the gospel, and our welcome into the family of God as a holy and chosen people were all designed to be *good news*. The kind of news you rejoice over, the kind that brings singing and laughter—because that's what God feels toward us:

> The Lord your God is in your midst,
> a mighty one who will save;

he will rejoice over you with gladness;
    he will quiet you by his love;
he will exult over you with loud singing.

—Zephaniah 3:17

God's love and His laughter are inseparable. His joy and holiness go hand in hand. And if we find these things in equal measure within the person of the Trinity, should we not pursue them in marriage?

The *Laughter* Experiment

Fortunately for me, Josh hasn't stopped telling jokes since we were engaged, so I've had plenty of time to adjust my feelings toward his humor. Perhaps the playfulness experiment helped too! Since he's the "punny" one, laughing at his jokes (or at least giving a sign I heard them, whether it was a jokingly annoyed expression or exaggerated sigh) was where I began.

Since Josh loves to crack jokes, though, it dawned on me how much fun he'd get out of *me* joking with *him*. I'd given him some books of dad jokes for Christmas, and I perused them for ideas. Then I waited for a good opportunity to sneak the puns into our daily life.

The first time I weaseled one of the jokes into our conversation, Josh was visibly surprised—and visibly proud. "That was a good one," he said, pleased with his influence. I tried a few more but felt that they were too rehearsed. Was it awkward? Yes! It's unnatural for me to think lightly; I'm too used to having my nose in a book. But I had to recognize that feeling awkward isn't the end of the world; it's the beginning of growth.

I changed things up and began watching for chances to litter our daily decisions—"Who will pick up groceries?" "Did you call the dentist?"—with lightheartedness. I'd make a pun out of his response. Or in a pause on a serious topic (not an argument; that would be ill timed) tell a knock-knock joke at random. For our specific relationship, this kind of spontaneity and humor is not normal coming from me. It made Josh laugh, which made me laugh, and there's nothing better than laughing together.

Your Flirtation Experiment

Maybe you're already the funny one in your relationship, and your husband has a different sense of humor. Maybe you already laugh together and are way ahead of me in this department. There are still ways you can cultivate lightheartedness and joy in a manner unique to your relationship. Maybe it's setting up a date to watch a movie that never fails to make your husband laugh (even if you hate it). Or maybe it's doing a silly dance in the kitchen because you're a terrible dancer, and he can't help but smile.

These things might not seem like the heavyweight actions of biblical joy. But if they draw you closer together, isn't that glorifying to God? Laughter bonds us with others. Shared laughter can bond you and your spouse in a special way, even if the activity isn't super spiritual. The spiritual impact on your relationship is still there regardless of how you facilitated it.

What would make you and your husband laugh? Where in your day can you weave some lightheartedness?

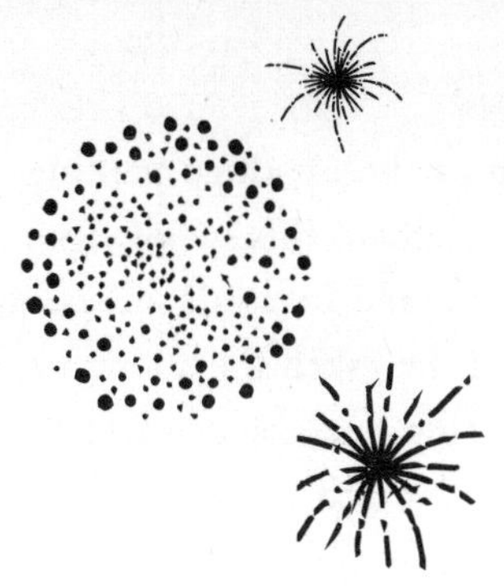

Chapter 8

Celebration

LISA

How such good news could spark such a falling out, I don't know. But it sure did. I had been working on a project for months and months, and we finally accepted an excellent offer from our first-pick publishing company. At this stage, it was a verbal agreement, and there were contract details to discuss, but we had landed the plane. After months of work going back and forth with our agent, we had an agreement, and I was on cloud nine.

That feels like a reason to celebrate, doesn't it?

That's what I thought too.

But Matt was upstairs in his office when the email confirmation came through, and so we resorted to a few short texts to acknowledge it was done at last.

Then *silence.*

Of course he must be up there making some kind of splendid plan for us to celebrate this major deal. I could hardly wait. At last, he came down, and I was all smiles. But he didn't mention the contract. Instead, he asked me about a small banking issue, a time-sensitive parenting decision, and something about stopping by Costco. That's it. No other acknowledgment of what had just occurred that morning.

And that hissing sound you're now hearing is probably the air escaping my party balloons. I didn't say anything. I *couldn't* say anything. Why had he communicated nothing about this amazing blessing and the most exciting news I had received in quite a while? *Nothing? Really?*

While waiting downstairs for Matt to announce his mind-blowing celebration plan, I had been messaging several close friends about the big news. And, oh, how they cheered! Lots of clapping hands and heart emojis. They were all in and as excited as I was, and more than a few included suggestions on the various ways Matt and I could celebrate this success. A night on the town? A bottle of champagne? My loving friends meant well but couldn't have known that those clapping emoji hands would soon turn to rubbing salt in a tender wound.

If it was so apparent to them what should be done about this momentous occasion, how could it possibly be lost on Matt?

And so I went from a thankful "Praise the Lord!" that morning to a raging "What is wrong with that man?" by the afternoon. Have you ever taken that journey? Doesn't take much time, does it? I was no longer focused on this marvelous answer to prayer; all I could think about was how much my husband's (lack of) response stole my joy.

The next time he came downstairs, I wasn't waiting for him to talk. I immediately dumped all my disappointment on him. Harsh words and angry tears poured out like a flash flood. He tried to interrupt with his side to the story, but I wasn't ready to listen. Two sides? Not to *this* story! I mean, really, how hard is it to celebrate a big win?

When I finished my tirade, he looked at me and quietly asked, "Babe, could I just say *one thing*?" I grabbed another handful of tissues and gave him that *whatever* look.

"Hon, I've been in the publishing business for over twenty-five years. I've seen many deals go sideways from the deal-points memo to the final contract. There's a lot of negotiating to do. Of course I'm happy we're this far, but I was planning to celebrate when the contract is signed."

In his mind this morning's news was a step in the process—an important step but only a step. Furthermore, he wanted to hold off until we could celebrate in a significant way, and due to our current circumstances, this was not possible. He is an all-or-nothing guy with a go-big-or-stay-home policy, and as you can tell, this was a "stay home" for him.

Oh, I wanted so badly to argue with him, and although he, evidently, wasn't seeing things as I saw them, he wasn't nearly as far out of line as I first believed. He just had a different perspective and a longer timeline. To his way of thinking, any serious celebration needed to wait for a final, signed contract.

By then I was so upset and emotionally spent that I despaired we'd do anything at all. Ever. "That's it. We're simply not good at celebrating—and probably never will be," I concluded. *Sniff.*

Matt didn't answer. Wise man.

Stopping to Celebrate

Celebration is an important part of life. We're quick to celebrate the birth of a child, a promotion at work, or a golden anniversary. It's not hard to see why such events would be exciting, and certainly worth celebrating.

But what about the other events in your marriage? Not merely the traditional ones—birthdays, promotions, or anniversaries—but different kinds of successes and momentous occasions. Do you stop to celebrate these? Maybe one of you completed a project you've been working on for a long time. Or perhaps you overcame a challenging hurdle or experienced a significant breakthrough. Had an unexpected answer to prayer.

Friends, this calls for a party. A victory dance. Or, at the very least, a fancy dessert.

And I'm not telling you this just because it's fun (although it's that too), but because we serve the God of celebrations. Throughout the Old Testament, God not only approves of such things but actually instructs His people to celebrate with music, songs, and festivals (Leviticus 23; Psalm 150; et al.). Consider King David, who broke out in dance when the ark finally arrived in Jerusalem.

In addition to the many Old Testament examples, you'll find plenty of celebrations in the New Testament as well. One of Jesus' best-known stories (Luke 15:11–32) ended in a huge celebration when the prodigal son returned and the father said, "Bring the fattened calf and kill it, and let us eat and celebrate" (v. 23). His first thought was to throw a delicious feast in celebration of the answer to his heartfelt prayers.

We serve the God of celebrations. . . . God not only approves of such things but actually instructs His people to celebrate.

So whatever you have going on in your life—what God has done for you or what He has brought you through—take a moment and throw a little (or a big) party!

The Celebration Experiment

You can guess I was glad to see the final contract arrive in the mail a few weeks after my little meltdown. I happened to be on my way to a mini writing getaway when it came in, so I took a quick minute to sign the papers and then hurried out the door.

But as Matt was loading up my suitcase in the car for me, I threw out an invitation to come see me that night. Although I made it sound spontaneous, the truth is I'd had this plan in mind for a while. My accommodations were rather charming and not far from home, so while I don't usually welcome company (not even his) during these retreats, I wanted to surprise him.

I didn't have to ask twice.

When Matt joined me that evening, we unloaded and unpacked, and eventually sat down on the window seat overlooking the pine trees. Then it was his turn to surprise me. From seemingly nowhere, he pulled out a golden bottle of champagne, popped the cork, laid out some gourmet chocolates, and we celebrated. He said it was "only a taste of what was to come" and didn't really count, but in my heart it certainly did.

Your Flirtation Experiment

Celebration is about remembering and reflecting on what is good. Is there a milestone ahead in the life of your marriage/husband/family? Have you experienced a breakthrough? A bright spot? An answer to prayer, big or small? These are all things worth celebrating.

Naturally there are all the regular days, but what if you chose a random evening, when your husband is least expecting it, to give thanks for the life you enjoy together? And if you're stumped as to what you might celebrate, set aside an hour or two to reflect on where God has brought your marriage—on the *great* things God has done for the two of you. Even if you've been through a heavy season, you're certain to find something good or beautiful for which you can be thankful.

Where should your next celebration be? A dinner in or out on the town, a walk by the river, a bicycle ride, a wilderness hike, a long drive in the country? You don't have to wait for him. Tell your husband you have something planned, and then celebrate the sweet things for which you're genuinely grateful.

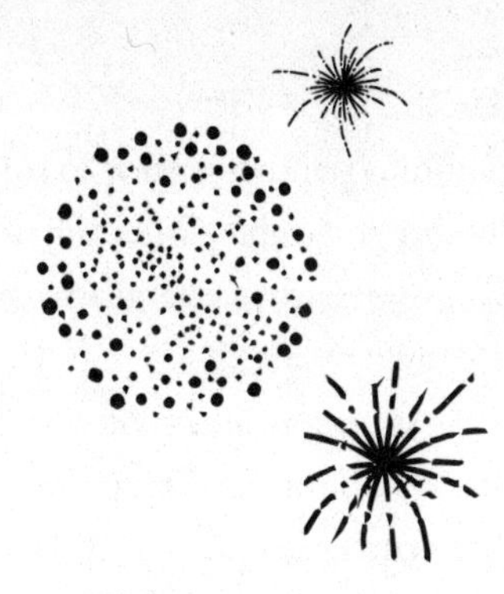

Chapter 9

Attraction

PHYLICIA

When I was almost twenty-two, I moved to Virginia to take a job at my alma mater. After an unsuccessful run at online dating, I shut down my profile and packed my bags for Lynchburg, hoping that, with my job change, I might meet a guy along the way. The chances were higher in a larger city, and I was excited to see what would happen.

My first week there, I met Josh in a bookstore parking lot—and I noticed him *not at all*. Let me rephrase: I noticed him, but not as any kind of dating prospect. And if you were to ask him about that meeting, he'd say the same thing about me.

We knew each other peripherally from then on, but neither of us was interested in the other. We just weren't that attracted, and both of us dated other people. Fast-forward six months and things had changed. Our platonic friendship grew to something more, and I found myself actually drawn to the gamer boy in green plaid shorts. And somehow he was interested in the girl with bad bangs and the worst eyebrow game known to man.

But even in the first few months of our dating relationship, we had some reservations about our attraction. We shared no hobbies. We had very different styles. We liked none of the same things. Everything the world told us was necessary for "chemistry" was in limbo for us. The question entered both our minds: *Do I stay, or do I go?*

We chose to stay. Some people would call it foolish; we called it a calculated risk. There was a chance our attraction could grow roots based on our shared values and time spent together. We took the chance. And we were right: the better we knew each other, the more we found to admire. And the more we admired each other's character, the more attracted we became.

A New Law of Attraction

I've never heard a marriage book discuss how attraction changes over the course of years—maybe I read all the wrong ones. No one told me that attraction, like sexual desire, can go up and down throughout the course of a marriage. It doesn't mean we love our husbands less or that they have failed in some area; it can be a response to stress. It can be the product of recent arguments and dissension. Attraction can fluctuate for many reasons, and contrary to what the world says, *lack of chemistry does not mean your marriage is over.*

***Attraction can fluctuate for many reasons, and contrary to what the world says,* lack of chemistry does not mean your marriage is over.**

There have been seasons in our seven years together when one or both of us didn't *feel* attracted. Whatever the reason—hormones, stress, busyness, fighting—I've learned that a momentary lack of spark doesn't mean we can't relight a fire.

Song of Solomon is the go-to when talking desire and Scripture, isn't it? We can quickly find evidence of the beauty of passion and attraction in the pages of this book. But we also see an interesting scene in Song of Solomon 5:2–6 that encourages me in seasons of distance:

> I slept, but my heart was awake.
> A sound! My beloved is knocking.
> "Open to me, my sister, my love,
>   my dove, my perfect one,
> for my head is wet with dew,
>   my locks with the drops of the night."
> I had put off my garment;
>   how could I put it on?
> I had bathed my feet;
>   how could I soil them?
> My beloved put his hand to the latch,
>   and my heart was thrilled within me.
> I arose to open to my beloved,
>   and my hands dripped with myrrh,
> my fingers with liquid myrrh,
>   on the handles of the bolt.
> I opened to my beloved,
>   but my beloved had turned and gone.

Early commentators and rabbis saw the Song of Solomon as an allegory of the relationship between God and Israel. But even if the book is allegorical, a human relationship is the picture used. This chapter shows us a difference of desire; the husband, in this case, is drawn to his wife—but she feels drawn to staying in bed. Been there? I have! If you continue reading the passage, by the time the wife's desire catches up with her, her husband is no longer at the door. I think modern lingo for this could be "two ships passing in the night."

Attraction can be mismatched. This is an ancient problem. But just because allure comes and goes doesn't mean we're captive to that roller coaster. The Shulamite woman did something intriguing: she proclaimed to other people all the things she admired about her spouse:

> My beloved is radiant and ruddy,
> distinguished among ten thousand.
> His head is the finest gold;
> his locks are wavy,
> black as a raven.
> His eyes are like doves
> beside streams of water,
> bathed in milk,
> sitting beside a full pool.
>
> —5:10–12

I'm not sure Josh would appreciate me saying his "eyes are like doves," but the principle still stands. Talking about his attributes—physical and otherwise—promotes attraction. I remember how when we were dating I would obsess over him to the point of distraction. Everything he did was *so great*. And when I remind myself of Josh's qualities in the midst of making sandwiches, scrubbing toilets, homeschooling, and running a business, I find myself more attracted to him.

But there's another piece to appeal: I find myself more open to the attractiveness of my husband when I *personally* feel attractive. There's a reciprocal nature to interest; in reaching out, I want to know I'll be received. And the more attractive I feel, the more confident I am to reach for him.

The Attraction Experiment

I'm not a Shulamite, but I relate to her experience. Working on attraction in seasons of difficulty, when we are indeed ships passing in the night, feels nonurgent and unnecessary. I would like to lie in my proverbial bed: "I've put off my garment, how can I put it back on?" In other words, *I've put on my sweatpants; how can I change?*

My attraction experiment had two angles. One focused on my inner dialogue about Josh. Instead of vocalizing the good things about Josh directly to him, I vocalized my love for Josh to *myself.*

As I washed the dishes: *Josh is so helpful with the kids. He is such a great dad.*

As we worked on taxes: *He is so smart with money. His skill is so attractive.*

As we traveled with our collection of little ones: *He's so patient in tough seasons.*

As we dressed up for an outing: *He gets better-looking with age.*

Some of this was vocalized to Josh, but most was kept to myself, a running dialogue of positivity.

The second piece of this experiment was about me *feeling* attractive. Postpartum, for me, means lots of spit-up, outfit changes, being at home, and quite honestly not looking or feeling beautiful. I'm a full-face-makeup girl who likes to get dressed for the day. But I'm also a work-at-home mom, and fancy outfits don't fit my current life stage. How could I both feel attractive and accomplish my day's work?

My solution was to invest in several sets of really cute, comfortable lounge sets, jumpsuits, and dresses. The dresses were casual enough to be worn at home and comfortable enough for sitting, cleaning, and schooling. The lounge sets and jumpsuits were several steps above my ancient black maternity sweats (which I wore while not pregnant, and which had a large hole on the thigh), fitted and in pretty colors, or with subtly sexy necklines that made me feel feminine and—if I'm being honest—regal.

Either of these experiments could have lit a spark on its own. But combining the two addressed both my mind and my emotions. Certainly my emotions could have changed by thinking positively about Josh, but by acting on my need to *feel* attractive, sparks flew a little faster.

Your Flirtation Experiment

Have you believed the lie that chemistry dies with marriage? There are definitely seasons when that can feel true; I've felt it myself. And undoubtedly our husbands have a role in this as well. Their reciprocation means the world.

I found, though, that taking steps to make my good marriage better by *thinking* about Josh's attractive qualities and *feeling* attractive myself naturally boosted the chemistry in our marriage. I may have started it, but Josh responded to it! Think about what might cultivate that response in your own relationship.

Maybe you feel the most chemistry with your spouse while doing an activity together. Could you set up a date to do that? Maybe you feel confident and sexy in jeans and a T-shirt from a concert you attended together years ago. Whatever works for you to encourage chemistry is a great starting point. For me, consistency was key. Cultivating attraction takes time, especially when you're out of the habit. The Shulamite ignored her husband's knocks repeatedly before finally getting out of bed to pursue him. Chemistry can take a little while—and that's okay.

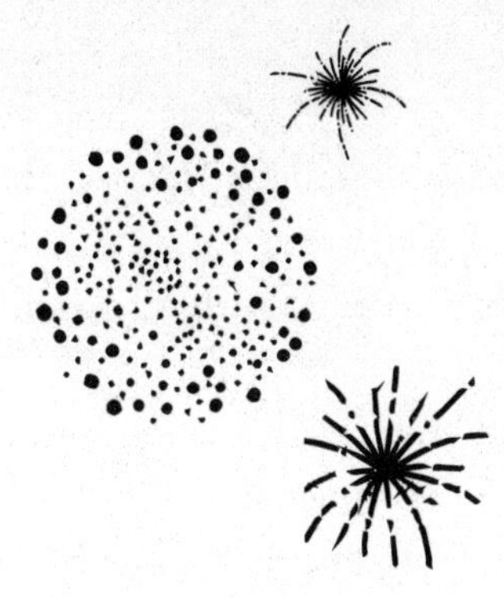

Chapter 10

Connection

LISA

I'm not clear, exactly, how it happened, but slowly, over the last year or more, Matt and I fell out of our healthier evening habits of reading books and turning in relatively early. This wasn't intentional; we just found ourselves so worn out and weary after we'd said our last goodnight to the kids that the only thing we were good for was watching a show or two (or five!) before switching off the lights.

"But, hey, we watch them together," we'd say to make ourselves feel better about this less-than-optimal routine. "Nothing wrong with a little veg-out," we'd add as he grabbed his computer and found the spot we'd left off in our latest series.

And it's true. I don't believe there's anything inherently wrong with watching an entertaining show to unwind from time to time.

But what had started as a small escape slowly became an hours-long nightly ritual for us. We were too tired to talk, too burned out to open a book. We just wanted to turn off our minds and turn on the screen.

But our evening binge wasn't as harmless as we first believed, because I found myself missing our end-of-the day conversations. Yes, we were both enjoying the same shows, but this kind of entertainment is hardly a satisfying substitution for heart connection. Yet what do you do when the day is done and you still have a couple of hours to kill before it's legit to hit the lights?

That's what kept me awake one night, well after we'd kissed goodnight. I tried to think back to *before*—back to when we'd begun our now nightly routine. What did we use to do? Matt and I both enjoy reading, so that was something we'd turn to—and share with each other—after our kids had gone upstairs. But currently? We still like to read, but we can't seem to keep our eyes open past a page or two.

All right, then what else? And that's when it came to me.

Games. We both grew up playing cards and board games. And so it was only natural for us to do the same after we were married. People seemed puzzled when we told them we'd packed Boggle (a fast-paced word game) for the Maui portion of our honeymoon. We played for hours on the balcony overlooking those white sand beaches. Crazy and a little competitive, but we loved it—and each other.

The morning following my sleepless night, I walked upstairs to search the game closet and, sure enough, found the Super Scrabble game. While this had never been my favorite game (it moves too slowly, and besides, Matt *always* wins), it seemed like the right choice for now.

That night after dinner, I suggested, "How about a rousing game of Scrabble?" He nodded, and we dusted off the box and started setting up the tiles. Only a few minutes later and we were back in the groove, playing the game for nearly two hours.

We laughed. We playfully argued. We debated over what counted as a real word (did you know that *aw* is in *The Official SCRABBLE Players Dictionary* and is worth five points?). We groaned when six of the seven tiles turned out to be vowels. And I let out a small shriek when he took over *my* triple word score with *glaze* (seventeen points multiplied by three!).

He won the game, just like old times. But somehow I didn't mind so much.

I loved that we went to bed with a fresh connection we hadn't felt in a while. Much of the richness of married life is found in the everyday routines of two hearts purposing to draw near to each other. But the years have revealed something that was not immediately apparent to me as a younger wife; I've discovered that it's often the woman who strongly pursues that "drawing near," proactively suggesting positive ways to connect.

Longing for Connection

Do you feel that yearning in your heart? We are women, uniquely created by God. It's only natural that we'd want this level of connection because God, in His creative wisdom and gracious goodness, chose to place this desire in our hearts. It is how we were made, right from the very beginning. When the desire for deep connection fills your thoughts, you are experiencing the authentic reality of how God designed you:

Then the man said,

"This at last is bone of my bones
  and flesh of my flesh;
she shall be called Woman,
  because she was taken out of Man."
—GENESIS 2:23

Adam, the first man (*ish*), awakened to discover this beautiful woman (*isshah*—"out of man") who was made from his very substance—from a portion of his body, removed from his side and fashioned into his wife by the hand of God. Everything about this momentous meeting shouted connection—linguistically, physically, and spiritually. These two were "one flesh" (2:24); two people, so close in every way that they were also *one single entity.*

When the desire for deep connection fills your thoughts, you are experiencing the authentic reality of how God designed you.

Is it any wonder that you look at that man across the room—your very own *ish* (how's that for a term of endearment?)—and desire a deeper connection?

The *Connection* Experiment

A while back, I heard an online writer friend talk about how she and her husband, while navigating rough waters in their community, had taken to show-binging in bed until they fell asleep. I didn't say anything to her back then, but I now confess that I silently disapproved of such a seeming waste of time.

Never realizing this would become Matt and me only a few years later.

Matt and I were both approaching what could well be called burnout and simply didn't want to think anymore. *Couldn't* think anymore. Getting lost in some other story than our own felt like a break for our minds.

This wasn't the end of the world. But it's not a place we wanted to stay either. We needed to get back to better habits and return to those activities that helped us connect before turning out the lights. The game of Scrabble might sound like an odd place to start, but it's been good for us. And since then we've learned a few new games, resumed reading, and added inviting friends over again in the evenings.

We also still watch a show from time to time. But we're determined to keep close and connected however we spend our evenings together.

Your Flirtation Experiment

If you're needing more connection, don't hesitate. Be enthusiastic and purposeful in taking that step. Don't wait for your husband to act, and don't wait until everything "clicks" back on its own (it won't); *just do it.*

Is there a game you both could play? An audiobook to listen to together? A new dessert recipe to try and for him to taste the results? Do you both enjoy music? Why not suggest you both pick out two songs to listen to together. After each song plays, share why you chose that song and why it's meaningful to you. Or perhaps he likes working out or jogging and wouldn't mind a gym buddy.

Set aside some time to brainstorm things that will bring connection to your heart and build relationship. Write out as long of a list as you can, including past activities and those on your would-be bucket list. Then pick one and start in.

You might want to give your husband a heads-up on what you're thinking to prepare him for your proposed change. But then again, you might not. Every husband is different, but Matt prefers I simply suggest a game to play than sit down and give him an hour of tearful thoughts on our terrible habits (inevitably translated, "You're not doing a good job in our relationship," even if we're both at fault).

Is your husband distracted, too busy, or simply unaware? Waiting around for his next move that may never come will only bring pain and resentment. Maybe he will come through, but why wait? Nowhere in the Bible are you told to be passive. You have no reason not to act, and there's no wisdom in waiting to initiate your desire for connection with him.

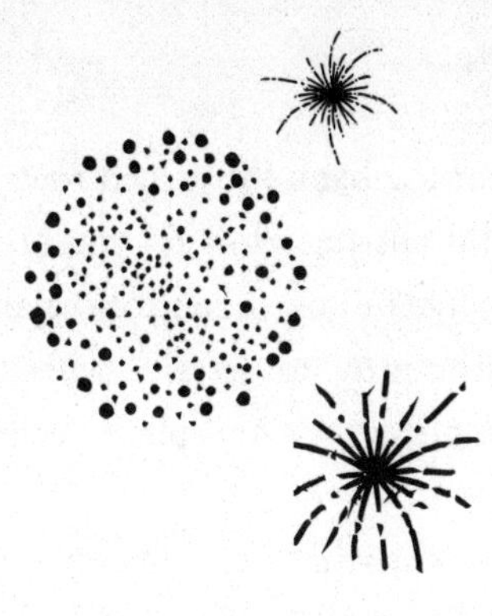

Chapter 11

Vulnerability

PHYLICIA

Days after our third child, Van, was born, I began having frenzied nightmares, sometimes before I was fully asleep. Between nursing sessions, in those precious minutes of sleep I needed so badly, the nightmares came swift and relentless. I would gasp awake, reaching for the bassinet to see if my baby was still breathing.

This wasn't the first time such nightmares occurred; I had similar experiences during and after both of my previous pregnancies. Sometimes they continued, although less often, into the toddler years. These terrors were not new, but I tend to keep quiet about my struggles. I'm not one to share my weakness, not even with those closest to me.

Not even with Josh.

But after two weeks, he could see something was going on. He'd hear the soft gasps as I woke up and stifled a cry. "Are you okay?"

he'd ask, reaching for the back I'd turned toward him. "I'm fine; it's just a bad dream," I'd answer. How do you bring a man into something so raw? And why couldn't I control the anxiety? Why couldn't I pray it away? I didn't want to describe what I saw, how every fear related to my children surfaced and played across my eyes whenever they closed.

He can't understand is what I told myself.

He won't respect this weakness is what I really felt.

Until one night, it was too much to hold in. I was scared to share my fear, but I also knew—as C. S. Lewis said—"to love at all is to be vulnerable."[5] Vulnerability was the risk worth taking.

"The nightmares won't stop," I whispered, hot tears dropping to my pillowcase in the dark. "They keep coming, and I'm so tired." The words did not come easily. I heard him turn toward me.

"When did this start?"

"The day after the baby was born," I said. I told him how they gripped me while he slept, how I couldn't rest between infant breaths, how fear and nighttime had become brothers. I opened the vulnerable place in my heart I'd tried to white-knuckle for years. And I cried—sobbed into his shoulder, streaking leftover mascara on our white duvet.

Community Requires Confession

James wrote to the community of faith on the importance of communal prayer and confession. When we hear "confession," our first thought is confession of sin, as James spoke of in James 5:16: "Therefore, confess your sins to one another and pray for one another, that you may be healed. The prayer of a righteous person has great power as it is working." But I believe the principle of confession applies to more than just sin. Confession of our sins, but also of our burdens, anxieties, fears, and trials, unites believers to one another and helps us to pray effectively. Being connected to this collective body of believers who support and encourage one another in pursuit of God is essential to the Christian faith.

In an equally yoked marriage, a marriage to a fellow believer (2 Cor. 6:14), a husband is also a brother in Christ. Passages regarding confession apply both to our church family and to our Christian marriage relationship. I don't know about you, but I tend to withhold some of my innermost struggles from my husband, saving them for my women's Bible study or a close girlfriend.

He won't get it.
I don't want to add to his plate.
He'll just want to fix me.

All these thoughts cross my mind. But I've discovered in the few years that I've been married that Josh wants to be invited into my vulnerable places. Seeing my weakness doesn't push him away; it actually invites him to be strong. More importantly, confession invites him to live out his responsibility as a Christian brother to bear my burdens (Gal. 6:2) and love me as Christ loves the church (Eph. 5:25–27).

Prayer, in particular, is an expression of love. I often picture intercessory prayer as a person standing in the throne room of heaven, bringing the needs of their loved one before the Lord. It's no coincidence that confession and prayer go hand in hand (see James 5 again). When we confess our sins or burdens to each other, the very best next step is to pray over those burdens. Ephesians 6:18 tells us to "[pray] at all times in the Spirit," to persevere in prayer and "[make] supplication for all the saints." Prayer is continual, sometimes difficult, and communal, and prayer between spouses can be a very vulnerable act. But in stepping out to confess and pray together, we are drawn toward the Lord and therefore toward each other.

My husband is not put off by my struggles. As he puts it, "When you are weak with me, you give me the chance to be your hero." When I block his chance to help, encourage, or pray for me because I (in pride) want to be the hero in my own story, I'm really trying to prove *I'm enough on my own*. But I'm not on my own—I'm married. And if he wants to love me in my weakness, we're both blessed when I give him the chance.

When we confess our sins or burdens to each other, the very best next step is to pray over those burdens.

The *Vulnerability* Experiment

This particular experiment was not planned. It was the outcome of a daily practice, consistently training myself to share more of my heart with Josh when I wanted to withhold. Without making pursuit of Josh's heart a priority, I find myself retreating into an ivory tower of emotional impenetrability. I had to overcome my natural tendency of concealing my feelings from Josh.

These natural tendencies to hold back serve me—and maybe you—well in some areas of life. Having command of my emotions helps me in the workplace or when dealing with confrontation. But what I call "strong" often comes across as unapproachable in my closest relationships. Josh feels unneeded, and while he may be appreciative of my actual strength, my lack of need translates as distancing myself from him. Confessing my heart's burdens on a regular basis—and particularly in that season of postpartum anxiety—closes the gap.

The night I cried into his shoulder, he gathered me in, stroking my hair with his free hand.

"God sees our children, babe," he whispered. "You can't control their safety, but He can."

Then, without being asked, he prayed over my heart, and I fell asleep.

Your Flirtation Experiment

If you're not in the habit of sharing your dreams, goals, burdens, or struggles with your spouse, this is going to be a challenging task. I relate. But I hope you've seen how letting your husband bear some of your burdens is a *Christian* practice, not just a marital one. Rather than agonize over how he will respond (or judge him when he does), set aside a time to get his full attention and share something you haven't shared with him before. It may be a dream you're thinking of pursuing, a goal you achieved and are super proud of, or a burden you haven't expressed.

He might not know how to deal with the information, and in that event, ask him to pray over you. As James said, "the prayer of a righteous person has great power." Your husband's prayers have great power in your life. Prayer is a vulnerable practice, but when we open the door to vulnerability in marriage, it is often reciprocated. Decide today what that will look like for you.

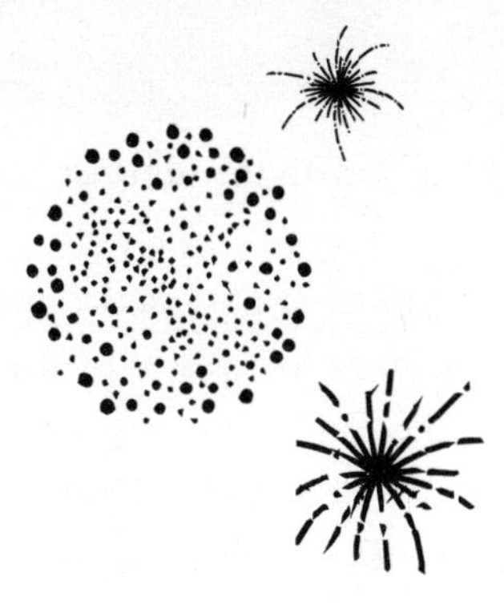

Chapter 12

Mystery

LISA

I began this particular flirtation experiment with such enthusiasm. We would have an evening to remember, and I knew just what we should do. The day would commence with clues written on small pieces of paper that would add to the mystery, then end with the grand finale of a special dinner together.

For once in our marriage, I would surprise Matt with a plan that he would never guess. I practically giggled at the thought—and I'm far past a giggling age!

So I mapped it all out. First, I called and made a reservation for two at 6:15 p.m. on Saturday, snagging one last spot at Zydeco on the Green, which offered a three-course dinner served out on the green under giant Ponderosa pine trees, complete with twinkly lights draped across the lawn and live music. It was the perfect romantic outdoor setting, late in the summer, just before the weather turned cool.

Next, I picked up cute little note cards, intending to leave Matt short, handwritten hints in various places throughout the day leading up to our big mystery date. Without giving Matt any further details, I told him I had dibs on him for Saturday night. He looked at me a little sideways from his chair with a suspicious, playful smile but agreed to go along with it.

That next morning came early. I found myself as nervous and excited as a young girl going out on her first date. I'm decidedly not a morning person, but I was having so much fun with this. Still sleepy, I fumbled around until I located the cards, and then, sitting down in my chair, wrapped in my blanket, I carefully opened the first card and wrote, "Dear Matt," . . .

Then I froze. I was totally frozen! Like Alaska, Siberia, and Greenland in winter frozen. Suddenly I felt ridiculous and couldn't do anything but stare at the fancy gold-rimmed card. *Why in the world did I think this would be a good idea? This is so stupid, stupid, stupid!* And the vigorous mental back-pedaling began in earnest. *Forget these goofy cards. He'll never know they had been part of the original mystery plan. What a juvenile idea. Let's just keep it to dinner.*

Within minutes, I went from "I'm so excited" to "Forget the cards" to "Cancel the reservation." *Is there a hole in the ground somewhere I can crawl in?* No, I wasn't done berating myself as I sat paralyzed in my chair. The "stupid" list continued like the end of a drum solo that won't stop. I now thought of everything that was so obviously wrong with my plan: Matt doesn't like dining outside (I know that. Why hadn't I factored that in?), the dinner will arrive cold, and the live music will be played by some amateur local bar band.

Stupid! Time to throw out the whole dumb plan.

I gritted my teeth and wrote, "Dear Matt," and made myself—I mean, *forced* myself—to write the next few words. Then I slipped the card onto the coffee tray and nervously waited for Matt's response when he opened the first envelope.

But he didn't laugh or tease. He smiled and was genuinely pleased with his first clue for our mystery date. "This is going to be fun. I'm looking forward to it!"

Whew! The weight lifted. Immediately, I smiled back at him and felt so much better, starting to count the hours until the end of the day.

Matt came out of the bedroom dressed and ready to go promptly at 4:30 p.m., and I handed him the second note card. This one gave driving directions to parking along the Deschutes River, where we walked beside the river together, holding hands, talking. In time we circled back to our car, where I gave him his next card—more driving instructions.

By then Matt was definitely into it and ready for whatever came next. We pulled into the golf course parking lot, where we soon could hear music playing and see the sparkly lights strung across the green. No more clues needed. All that was left to do was sit back and enjoy the wild-caught salmon dinner (served piping hot!) under the deepening night sky and, after dinner, hold each other, listening to the (reasonably talented) folk musicians from Nashville.

The Mystery of Marriage

How do you explain a man and a woman falling in love? You can't, although the poets and writers of love songs never cease to try. Remember (in Phylicia's preface) what Solomon, in all his wisdom, wrote in Proverbs 30:18–19:

There are four things that are too mysterious for me to understand:

> an eagle flying in the sky,
> a snake moving on a rock,
> a ship finding its way over the sea,
> and a man and a woman falling in love. (GNT)

As fantastical as it sounds, I fell in love with Matt the moment he walked through the door at that first small dinner party. I could tell you exactly what he was wearing that night, the questions he asked me, and how hard he made me laugh over that wild, boys versus girls card game. I left our friends' house that evening convinced he was the man I would marry. It took him three days longer to reach the same conclusion (I don't know why it took him so long!).

And to this day, I couldn't tell you *why*. Just that it was. It remains a mystery.

But there's another kind of mystery when it comes to a Christian marriage, voiced by the apostle Paul in Ephesians 5, and rather than talking about something hidden and incomprehensible (like falling in love), this mystery is about something beautiful and *revealed*.

> Husbands, love your wives, as Christ loved the church and gave himself up for her, that he might sanctify her, having cleansed her by the washing of water with the word, so that he might present the church to himself in splendor, without spot or wrinkle or any such thing, that she might be holy and without blemish. In the same way husbands should love their wives as their own bodies. He who loves his wife loves himself. For no one ever hated his own flesh, but nourishes and cherishes it, just as Christ does the church, because we are members of his body. "Therefore, a man shall leave

> his father and mother and hold fast to his wife, and the two shall become one flesh." *This mystery is profound*, and I am saying that it refers to Christ and the church.
>
> —VV. 25–32

In this extraordinary passage, believers learn that marriage isn't what we are doing or have chosen to do. Our marriage is what God is doing in the world for His purposes. The revealed mystery of your marriage and mine is that our love and relationships are to be a reflection to the watching world of how Jesus Christ loves His bride, the church.

As we pursue closeness and connection, and enliven the fires of our marriages with the coy fun of mystery, let's also remember that the closer and more loving we are, the more accurately we reflect to the world the perfect love Jesus Christ has for His church.

The revealed mystery of your marriage and mine is that our love and relationships are to be a reflection to the watching world of how Jesus Christ loves His bride, the church.

The *Mystery* Experiment

How easy I presumed this experiment would be. A planner by nature, I've put together numerous—and far more complicated—events. How difficult could it be to plan out a mystery date?

And the planning really was easy. What I didn't anticipate was that initial morning panic. In those early hours, I grew worried that Matt might think this was a sappy idea. Or that he wouldn't enjoy the evening. Despite being married for twenty-eight years (decades!), all my girlish insecurities came back to haunt me—nearly keeping me from making a romantic move on my very own husband.

Looking back, I'm pleased I proceeded with the plan, despite how ridiculous I felt. As the day progressed, confidence grew, and I enjoyed teasing Matt with my secret clues and small surprises along the way.

As for Matt, although naturally the guy in charge, he seemed quite content to let me take the lead on this one. That part was unexpected. He truly was a good sport, even dressing the way I'd instructed and waiting patiently for each clue as it came.

As the night air progressively encouraged us to sit closer, we soon found ourselves snuggling together under the provided blankets, listening to the musicians sing just about every love song we knew late into the night. A sensation of warmth and happiness swept over me as the evening came to a close.

Your Flirtation Experiment

Are you ready to step away from the everyday and keep your husband guessing, but you don't know where to begin? Is the prospect of creating something from scratch daunting? If so, you can still enjoy a splendid mystery evening by doing a little research. A quick internet search will turn up articles such as "101 Mystery Date Ideas" for all kinds of creative options. Even if you don't end up going with one of those ideas, they might inspire you to come up with a variation of your own.

If you're feeling even more ambitious, another fun idea is attending—or hosting—a murder mystery party. Our daughter threw one of these a few years ago, and it was a huge hit with everyone who attended (Matt was the butler, and I was the maid—complete with costumes).

Depending on where you live, many towns offer a mystery dinner or mystery theater, which can be great fun as well.

Then again, you can always keep it simple, as I did, and write down a handful of clues and find your way to the park (or movies, dinner, and so forth) together. The mystery of the journey matters far more than the destination!

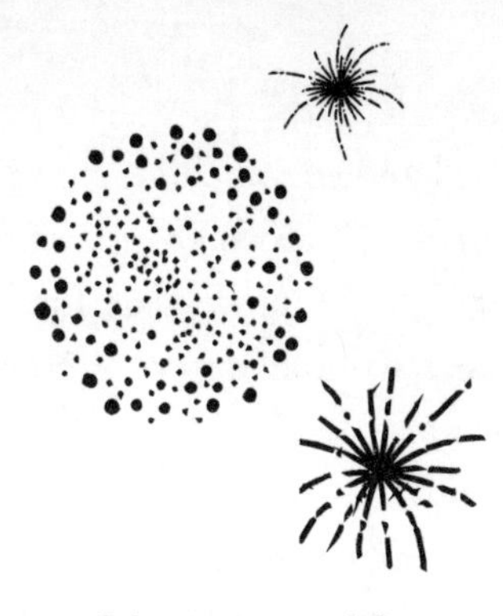

Chapter 13

Affirmation

PHYLICIA

I don't know *whose* idea it was to start potty training our middle child when our third was barely three weeks old, but it seemed like a great concept at the time. Avoid potential potty regressions, train her while we are all home with the baby—what's not to like?

Clearly, someone (*ahem*, me) didn't think it through. Three days in, Josh and I were exhausted by a newborn sleep schedule *and* cleaning up potty accidents in every corner of the house. On top of that, our oldest started acting out in ways we'd never seen before. Only three weeks into three children, and it felt like a three-ring circus!

We tried hard not to snap at each other, but the exhaustion, accidents, disciplining, and every-two-hour feedings took their toll. I found myself judging Josh's parenting from my perch in the nursing chair, annoyed that he handled *this* child *that* way. All the wonderful things he'd done to make my postpartum season peaceful? I forgot them. All I saw was room for improvement. I mulled on his transgressions until they became a veritable stew of offenses in my mind: *he should have; why didn't he? I wish he'd . . .*

Keeping this mental tab of Josh's failings, things I wished he would change or do better, began as a bad habit in seasons of stress. I did my best not to say anything, but inevitably my dissatisfaction manifested on my face.

"What's wrong?" Josh would ask.

"Nothing," I'd lie.

"Then why are you looking at me like that?"

Mental tab became verbal volcano, and all those stuffed-in feelings flowed like lava from my mouth. Josh was often burned in the process.

Then it dawned on me: What if, instead of a list of what Josh did *wrong*, I made a list of what he'd done *right*? Not just "right" according to my standards, but genuinely good, helpful, admirable things. If my mental tab of negativity was making me angry and dissatisfied, could a mental tab of positive thoughts about my husband make me more pleasant? Could it make me like my husband more?

I tried it. Every time a negative observation popped into my brain, I added a positive one.

I wish he'd notice the dishes before they're piled on the counter . . . but *he lined up all the insurance details for us this month.*

It took a few days, but it changed me. Sure, I still noticed the dirty dishes. But I was quicker to see his hard work for the family or how he involved our daughter in his chores or how he thought to bring me my water bottle without my asking. They were little things, things easy to take for granted, but evidence of his care.

The Power of the Mind

The power of our thoughts is not a new concept. Scripture emphasizes the influential nature of the mind, most famously in Paul's letter to the Philippian church: "Finally, brothers, whatever is true, whatever is honorable, whatever is just, whatever is pure, whatever is lovely, whatever is commendable, if there is any excellence, if there is anything worthy of praise, think about these things" (Phil. 4:8).

Thoughts guide actions. Thinking about honorable things leads to honorable choices. Thinking about justice leads to just behavior. Thinking on what is pure protects against depravity. Patterns of thought shape our character, and since our character should be the image of Christ, our thoughts should be "on things above, where Christ is" (Col. 3:1–2 NIV).

In another letter, Paul exhorted his protégé Timothy to embrace a spirit "of power and of love and of a sound mind" (2 Tim. 1:7 NKJV). There is a connection between our strength, our love for others, and the thoughts we think. We shouldn't be surprised that negative, brooding thoughts limit our patience (strength for relationships) and our love (heartfelt appreciation for others), especially regarding a spouse.

Science supports what Scripture teaches: positive thoughts can help treat mental health conditions, lower stress, boost academic achievement, and more. And that's when the thoughts are focused on *self.* When such positive thoughts are focused on another person's good qualities, they may produce a similar transformation. Speaking affirmation over oneself boosts confidence. Couldn't affirmation of a spouse accomplish something similar in a wife's estimation of her husband?

I've often found myself noticing good things about strangers—their cute earrings, pretty hair, or adorable baby. I was once advised,

"Never miss an opportunity to give a compliment," and so I've tried to make a point of affirming the beautiful things I see in people. If it's easy to do in the Walmart checkout line, why is it so hard at home? Probably because we don't see the flaws and errors of the woman in the checkout line, but with our husbands, we most definitely do. It's easier to compliment someone who has never inconvenienced us than to choose daily to see good in the sinner under our own roof.

Affirming good in others starts with how we think about them. Philippians 4:8 works well as a guide: Is this thought true of my husband? Is this thought honorable? Is it just and fair? Is it commendable, pure, or praiseworthy? If not, why am I dwelling on it?

This doesn't mean we ignore real sin issues in our husbands. One of the great gifts wives bring to marriage in our *ezer* (strong help, military aid) role is discernment and counsel. A good marriage is iron sharpening iron (Prov. 27:17). But in between those blacksmithing moments, how we think about our spouses molds both us and them. What we affirm in our husbands can build trust in our counsel or can make them feel as though we don't like them at all.

Affirming good in others starts with how we think about them.

The *Affirmation* Experiment

Thinking well of Josh was a noble start, but my thoughts were private (a good thing when they were negative!). The effort needed a further step, expressed not just to myself but also to Josh. I noticed Josh's effort and character but missed the opportunities to compliment him.

One afternoon as he held our infant, Van, while I folded laundry on the sofa, I told him, "I have something for you."

"Oh, what?" He looked up from his phone.

I pulled out my own device and opened Google Docs. "It's a letter," I said. "I know you're not much of a words person, but I wanted to tell you some things I've noticed about you lately."

He was curious now. I cleared my throat and read the letter aloud:

> You have made my life easier and this postpartum so much better than I could have hoped. Breakfast in bed? Taking the baby in the night so I can sleep? You protected my health when I wasn't good at protecting it myself. The girls got to spend more time with you, and that's a gift to them.
>
> I know that this season can be frustrating and hard to deal with at times, especially with parenting—but you are patient and kind with the girls, and that's what they need from their daddy in order to be strong women someday. I am glad I could entrust them to you while recovering and while working on the business.

As I shared other things I appreciated—his time in the Word, often done on his Bible app with a baby in one arm and toddler on a potty at his feet—his face softened, and I could tell he felt seen. His work wasn't going unnoticed or underappreciated.

"Can you send that to me?" he said softly when I finished reading.

Your Flirtation Experiment

Words of affirmation might not be your husband's love language, but he will still appreciate hearing what you've noticed about his character, work, and heart. I chose to write my letter out and read it aloud, but you might make a list of your husband's qualities and write him a note a day, packed in his lunch. Or maybe you could text them to him.

As you consider your own affirmation experiment, remember that focusing on the good doesn't mean your husband never fails. I'm not suggesting we suspend rationality! But I discovered that replacing negative patterns of thought with positive affirmations changed not only my perspective of him but made him want to grow even more.

What will you do today to affirm your spouse?

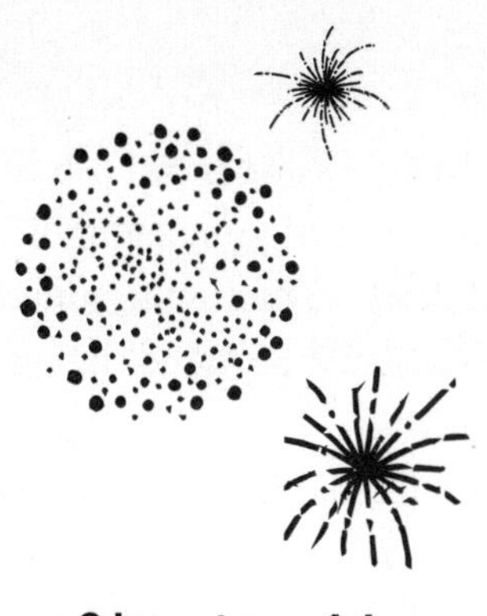

Chapter 14

Refuge

LISA

Matt's boyhood adventures are the stuff of legend in our home. How he moved with his parents from Oregon to the interior of British Columbia and at the age of ten was required to walk to the bus stop a mile from the house in twenty-nine-degrees-below-zero weather; how he went moose and bear hunting with his brother and father and went whitefish and salmon fishing in the Fraser River; and how he was given his own horse as a young boy will forever be told in the accounts of our family's history. A wild, tough, thrilling childhood, if ever there was one.

For much of the summer, Matt would take off on his horse and be gone all day—sometimes with his sister, sometimes alone—not returning until dinnertime or dark—an extraordinary amount of independence for a ten-year-old kid. Our children would listen, wide-eyed, to his adventure stories of bush life, visibly longing for such freedom as their dad had growing up. If only they could have their own horse and disappear for hours and days like he did! Matt certainly enjoyed an unusual boyhood, living out his very own *My Side of the Mountain*.

And I, too, envied his childhood adventures and wondered what it must have been like to take off like that without a care in the world. Having grown up in the suburbs of Southern California, I had an entirely different experience. *I could only imagine.*

But marriage affords an insider's perspective, enabling spouses to have an up-close view into each other's soul. For some years I was puzzled by certain aspects of Matt's way of being. Someone could drive a truck through the living room and he wouldn't flinch but would only be concerned that no one was hurt. Conversely, something that seemed so small to me triggered a visceral response in him.

One day my inklings gained perspective. What had been blurry came into clear definition. Was all that freedom positive? I used to think so.

We had a young friend over visiting, a darling ten-year-old boy, and I found myself carefully keeping an eye on him. Not that I thought he'd get into any trouble, but our small acreage is surrounded by many more acres of wide-open land, and I worried he'd wander off or get hurt. Chalk it up to basic maternal instinct.

And in that maternal moment, it struck me like a hard punch to the gut. This young boy whose safety I was so concerned about was the exact same age as Matt was when he was out riding his horse alone day after day, unsupervised, in the bush. I couldn't stop thinking about this little ten-year-old visitor; I wouldn't let him walk unaccompanied a half mile down to the mailbox, let alone leave in the early morning on a horse, only to return near dark. Suddenly those amazing childish adventures didn't seem quite so wonderful anymore—to me they sounded simply awful, neglectful, and even dangerous.

I didn't say anything at the time, but a few days later I brought up the topic with Matt. "You know your stories of riding your horse all day alone, without so much as a cell phone?" Not waiting for an answer and with a shaking voice, I continued, "Who was taking care of you, looking after you?"

He said nothing for a few seconds, but powerful emotion found the silence, turned his eyes to the past, and pushed its way into that moment. "I was a lost boy . . . totally alone."

My suspicions were confirmed at that moment. I instinctively knew all that freedom for so young a boy couldn't be all good. "Freedom" could just as well have been called "forgotten." The amazing aspect of such a unique life can't be denied, but in part, that's what that extraordinary freedom turned out to be. Matt's young boy's heart lived with the belief that he mattered to no one. We both grieved over what was lost and what should not have been.

How strange yet beautiful to stumble upon an old, deep wound hidden for decades and to be trusted with it by my husband.

A Place of Refuge

Naturally Matt's childhood experiences have spilled over into our own relationship, as have mine. How could they not? No wonder he felt the need to protect his heart. Now I understand, more than ever, why I need to communicate that I'm here for him, that I'm loyal, and that I care for those sacred, tender places in his heart that the Enemy has handled with such callous disregard.

But my husband isn't the only one. We all long for a refuge, somewhere to go where danger and distress are banished. *Someone* who will be steadfast and sure. A shelter in the storm.

> For he will hide me in *his shelter*
> *in the day of trouble*;
> he will conceal me under the cover of his tent;
> he will lift me high upon a rock.
>
> —Psalm 27:5

> Trust in him at all times, O people;
> pour out your heart before him;
> *God is a refuge* for us.
>
> —Psalm 62:8

A refuge is a sanctuary—a place where mercy is extended and grace is offered. That has a familiar ring to it, doesn't it? God is the shelter from life's storms for everyone who believes, which is why we have what it takes as Christian wives. We've been given what we are called and commissioned to give away—the grace we have received. Where love is consistently given in the form of mercy and grace, the walls come tumbling down.

What does it mean to be a refuge for your husband's heart? It means that you are safe, that he can come to you, that you'll be there for him, and that you're holding strong. Whatever else may be happening out in this harsh world we live in, he can count on you for comfort, trust, and love. Your heart is his safe place.

Are you a place of refuge for your husband? Are his deepest wounds safe in your keeping?

A refuge isn't built overnight, for it takes time to create that kind of confidence, and if trust has been broken in your husband's life—by you or by someone else—then it will likely take longer. But you can begin by telling him that you want to be his safe place from now on.

MATT

> Everyone thought I was so tough, so self-sufficient, that I didn't need anything or anyone. While I simultaneously loved my wild freedom when so young, I also silently felt like I mattered to no one, and that little boy remained inside the man he became a few years later. The voices of childhood are so powerful. I thank God, through Jesus Christ, for the refuge He gives and for the wife who blesses me, caring for the secret places of my heart.

The Refuge Experiment

Life makes a refuge out of many things. When Matt was a young, lonely boy, his horse was that refuge. Although horses have always been a big part of Matt's life, it's been a while since he has had the opportunity to ride, having given up our horses when our daughter developed severe allergies. Our own small stable has been empty for years, the six stalls now used for storage rather than hay or horses. But I thought, *Wouldn't it be fantastic if I could get Matt out on a ride again?*

One of our daughters came up with a solution, having made friends with a manager at Brasada Ranch, not far from where we live. She connected us, and from there I was able to arrange an outing for Matt.

Matt and I like doing many things together, but not this time. For one, I knew I'd hold him back; and second, I'm not too excited about horses or riding. But I did send him off with my love. And told him

I'd be waiting for him when he got back and would want to hear all about it. How it made me smile to see him back on a horse! He was smiling too.

Your Flirtation Experiment

Take a moment to reflect on what being a refuge might look like in your marriage. How can you communicate to your husband that you're committed to being that safe place for him—a place where he can be secure even when his defenses are down?

Have you ever had that conversation? You could choose a special evening to tell him directly that you always want to be a shelter for him, a place of refuge. Or maybe you can write it in a note and leave it on his desk or his pillow.

Sometimes important conversations can be made more enduring by a particularly memorable experience that speaks to that place of retreat, comfort, and sanctuary. You can also create a moment right in your own home, a cozy spot for the two of you where you can go to talk and cuddle. Carve out a corner of your bedroom or arrange for a sweet spot on the patio or porch. It's not difficult to arrange. Whether your husband is a complicated or a simple man, just tailor the experience to who he is.

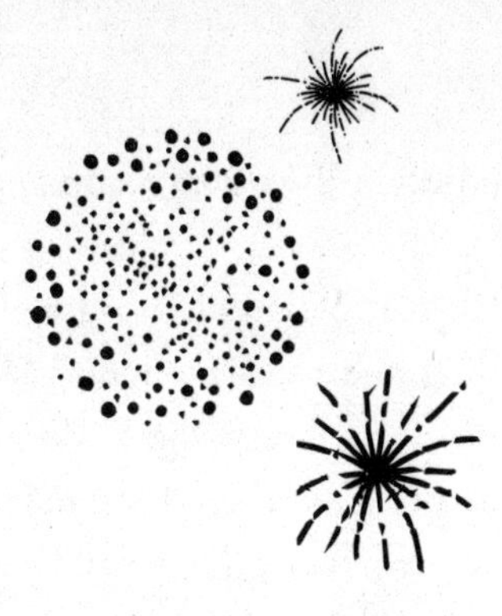

Chapter 15

Friendship

PHYLICIA

"I didn't come to marriage looking for a best friend."

The words flew out of my mouth before I could stop them, and Josh looked at me, stunned. It was our first year of marriage, and we were in another fight over yet another miscommunication—we seemed to rotate through the same ones—and the words were flying fast and hot. I didn't care how my words made Josh feel. I just wanted to protect my independence.

Josh and I married in a college town surrounded by Christian twentysomethings who all seemed to write their vows the same way. At some point after the rope twisting or sand pouring or foot washing, husband and wife would both tearfully confess how lucky they were to marry their best friend. I heard this enough in real life and

Hallmark movies to decide, *I have no desire to marry my best friend, whatever that even is.*

In my twenty-four-year-old mind, the idea of marrying one's "best friend" was suffocating and claustrophobic. *One* best friend? I had dozens of friends, never a solitary "best" one. To marry your best friend meant losing all other ones, and I wanted none of that. I wanted marriage, but I also wanted to preserve my independence—at all costs.

The cost was high, and I paid the price. My idolatry of independence made marriage to Josh rocky and painful. What he believed thoughtful, I believed clingy. What he considered friendship, I considered codependence. The closer he got to me, the further I pulled away. Instead of coming to marriage to build something good and new, I came to it avoiding what I didn't want—an unhealthy, codependent marriage like the ones I'd observed as a single person. I knew what I was *against*, but I had no idea what I was *for*, and this shaped our relationship into a cold commitment of separate hobbies, activities, and social circles. The impact of those first two years reverberated through our marriage long after they were over.

Building friendship into my marriage has been a long-term process that even a Flirtation Experiment couldn't expedite. But the Experiment met me at a good time in our relationship, a time after I had laid friendly groundwork, worked on my attitudes and idolatries, and become closer to Josh than before. This inner work was necessary for me to take the more visible steps of not just being friendly but becoming his friend.

I Have Called You Friends

Friendship is risky. If you've ever been through a friendship breakup, you know how painful they can be. Friendship is an unspoken contract of love and goodwill. C. S. Lewis described it well in *The Four Loves*: "When two such persons discover one another, when . . . they share their vision—it is then that Friendship is born."[6]

Shared vision and purpose, the sense of "me too!" between people, unforced and not coerced—this is the stuff that makes a friendship. More than that, friendship looks out for the good of the other, and the ultimate act of friendship is to lay down your life for your friend (John 15:13). Giving up your most precious commodities—your time, attention, or life itself—is the fullest form of friendship and truest form of love.

It was no small thing, then, for Jesus to say, "I no longer call you servants, because a servant does not know his master's business. Instead, I have called you friends, for everything that I learned from my Father I have made known to you" (John 15:15 NIV).

The almighty God incarnate, owing humanity nothing and yet giving everything, was willing to call us *friends*. Jesus' relationship with us was a risk of eternal proportion. In loving us and inviting us to love Him, He knew many would choose not to do so (Matt. 22:14). And because we are His friends, we are given an inside look at His redemptive plan. We are not forced to be the friends of Christ, but we are invited to be friends by His love. We are invited into His purpose.

If the God of the universe stoops to offer friendship to humans—"unsafe" as it is—it is worth considering the importance of friendship to another covenant relationship: marriage. Friendship between humans is interdependent. It requires trust and sacrifice. These are hard to offer when we remain bound by past trauma and childhood hurts; we can't pour from an empty vessel. Until we deal with our aversion to the vulnerability that friendship requires, our marriage relationships will remain surface and separate. Jesus gives us a template for friendship in

Until we deal with our aversion to the vulnerability that friendship requires, our marriage relationships will remain surface and separate.

marriage, and it doesn't require a mutual passion for the same '90s grunge music or Die Hard movies or presidential biographies. This kind of friendship can happen even without those peripheral interests. It's a friendship based on love for *the person himself.* It's a reminder of who he is as an image bearer of God.

The Friendship Experiment

I remember making a "future husband list" as a teenager, a list I cringe to behold today (I still have it!). Among the silly requirements for hair color and height, I had listed "likes to ski." If I had married a fellow Michigander, that would have been easy enough, but Josh is from Virginia. Imagine my good fortune to discover that Josh grew up by a ski resort—just like me—and enjoyed it just as much as I did. But skiing isn't easy with small kids. Particularly with babies.

I am sure I could have settled for an at-home date, but when you work at home and homeschool, being home is incredibly overrated. No, I needed a date that we both would enjoy, one that required us to *engage* in the activity. Skiing is one of those activities for us. I chose one of our local resorts and arranged for two of the kids to be with our sitter and one to go to my mom's and booked the lift tickets.

The day arrived, and our excitement was tangible. I could sense how thrilled Josh was to get outside with me. The wind bit our faces as the ski lift whisked us up the hill, and memories of our first anniversary came rushing back with it.

Six years earlier, Josh had planned a trip to Snowshoe in West Virginia. We were so excited to get away from work, even though I was finishing my degree and had to bring homework along. The ski conditions were perfect that first day, and we took advantage of every minute outdoors. I still have a picture of us standing at the top of a lift, the mountains rolling behind us like a wrinkled blanket, black and white.

That night I didn't feel well. I'd been extremely tired—I chalked it up to late nights doing homework and full days at my job—but I was nauseous too.

"I'm going to take a pregnancy test," I announced, leaving my laptop open to the quiz I was taking. Josh rolled his eyes and laughed.

"You take a pregnancy test *every* month."

He wasn't wrong—I was a paranoid newlywed. But this time I was convinced something was up. I took the test, set it on the counter, and ran back to my computer.

"Aren't you going to look at it?" Josh asked, peering into the bathroom.

"Maybe in a minute." I answered another quiz question, pretending to be focused, but I was freaking out inside. "Actually"—I turned around—"you can look at it."

He walked into the bathroom and stood still, his back to me. He turned around and—you guessed it—two pink lines.

Fast-forward six years to another ski lift in another state, and those two pink lines had turned into three sweet babies, a farmhouse, a family business, and . . . a best friendship. I tapped Josh's ski with a pole.

"I'm glad I get to do life with you."

He smiled. "Me too."

Your Flirtation Experiment

No two friendships are the same. When I think about my friendships with women (like Lisa!) the diversity is evident. The same goes for marriage: your friendship with your spouse is unique and special. What makes you look at him and say, "Me too"?

For us, it's skiing and working out. For you, maybe it's that playlist of music you both loved in high school. Maybe it's a team you're both rooting for or a rivalry that brings out your sass. What is it about your relationship with your husband that makes you feel like he shares your vision and values? How could you invest in that?

Perhaps you're like I was in those early days. Perhaps you feel as if befriending your spouse leads to codependency, and dependence only leads to hurt. Maybe you keep him at an arm's length to protect yourself emotionally; you're not used to opening up. He's a friend from whom you've drifted. What could bring you closer again?

This experiment assumes that your husband is a good man who is not abusing or manipulating you in any way. Please see page xxii of "Before We Begin" for more details.

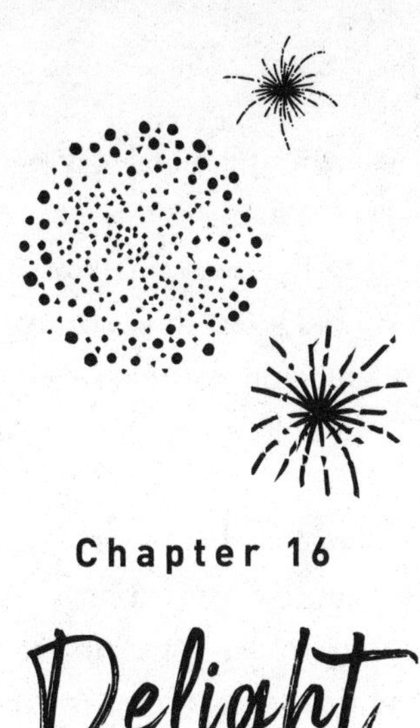

Chapter 16

Delight

LISA

The two were newlyweds, so it was no surprise that they would still be so wrapped up in each other. Some people found it a bit too much—the way they couldn't keep their eyes, or hands, for that matter, off of each other—but I thought it was awfully sweet to see.

One Sunday things were different. She arrived at church alone, looking a little lost. It turned out her husband had been called out of town for work.

But toward the end of the service, he arrived, and oh, if only you could have seen her face when he walked in. He tried to enter discreetly, but her beaming expression announced to the entire room that Dwight had arrived at last. I think he must have been a little embarrassed, but in a good way—the kind when a man knows the whole world is aware that he is one very loved man.

And I couldn't help smiling along, giving my husband a slight nudge so he could enjoy the moment too.

Looking over at Matt, however, I was rather startled by his expression. Let's just say it was less than positive. I didn't understand. Didn't he approve? What could possibly be his problem? Why didn't he find it endearing, as I did? Was that a vague sense of sadness on his face?

When we were alone later that night, I turned to question him about that earlier moment. He assured me that he was indeed quite happy for them; his mind was on something else.

Have you ever had that sense of dread that you might be part of the explanation? "It doesn't have anything to do with *me*, does it?" I asked, but I already guessed the answer.

"I was just thinking . . . I sometimes wish you'd light up like that when you see *me*." And he said it so wistfully that I couldn't even pretend to misunderstand his meaning.

I knew there was truth in what he was saying. I knew it—and I hated it.

For whatever reason, I rarely "lit up" for my husband anymore. Which actually made no sense, because we had a good marriage, felt close, and expressively loved each other every day. Perhaps it was because we saw each other all the time and the newness had (understandably) worn off long ago.

Or maybe it was because I'd already given out all my smiles to our children throughout the day.

Or perhaps it was because I'd grown overly complacent with the very same man who used to send me sailing by simply walking into the room.

I knew it didn't really matter though. I recalled how my girlfriends used to tease that they could always tell the minute when Matt had arrived—not by watching the door but by watching my face. They said my smile announced his presence better than any bell.

So what happened to that young woman who was me?

Nothing—and *everything.* Daily life with babies and homeschooling, music lessons and ministry meetings, breakfast, lunch, and dinner. Somehow it had all stacked up, and without my even realizing it, I'd stopped smiling *like that.*

And I hadn't fallen out of love or anything. Quite the opposite; our love was deeper than it had ever been in our first year together. But I no longer took the trouble to communicate my happiness, not so much as offering a bright smile at the sight of Matt. As painful as it was to have it pointed out, it certainly wasn't how I wanted it to be with us.

Delighting in the One You Love

Often when we think about biblical marriage our minds run to all the *shoulds* and *sacrifices*—and there's much to be said for those things—but let's not lose that sense of *delight* God intends for us to enjoy as well.

Hardly subtle, you'll see the theme of delight scattered throughout the Bible, and nowhere is it more ardently expressed than in the sensuous poetry of the Song of Solomon. "Behold, you are beautiful, my beloved, truly *delightful*" (1:16). And again, only a few verses later: "With great *delight* I sat in his shadow" (2:3).

Reading these words, you can practically see the Shulamite *beaming* with love and pleasure. This woman is unabashed in her delight for her lover.

Then, when you get to chapter 3, this same woman has a strange, bad dream where she is looking for her lover throughout the city and can't locate him anywhere. You can almost feel her panic when he is nowhere to be found. Then, as her desperate search continues, she asks the watchmen if perhaps they've seen him. And it's barely a minute or two later when, to her great relief, she finds him—*him whom her soul loves*: "Scarcely had I passed them [the watchmen] when *I found him whom my soul loves*" (v. 4).

I love this part of the story. It's a Hallmark moment if ever there was one. "I held him, and would not let him go" (3:4). Can't you just picture this joyous reunion? She thought she might have lost the man she loves, and suddenly he's happily in her arms again!

Now let's revisit those newlywed friends. How similar to this scene from the Song of Solomon was their delight in each other. I had to ask myself what my face should look like upon suddenly finding "the one whom my soul loves." How warm should my smile be then? *At least* as sunny as a newlywed spotting her husband entering church an hour or so late.

Needless to say, we don't need to break down in sobbing ecstasy every time our men walk into the room. But how about loving eyes and a brightness in your smile that says, *Oh, it's* you*—the man I love. You're here, and I couldn't be happier*?

The *Delight* Experiment

Soon after that *enlightening* conversation with Matt, I purposed that if I was going to "light up" for anyone, it would be for him. Yet I knew I couldn't count on fuzzy feelings and a vague promise to do better. I needed to come up with a concrete "you light up my life" plan.

My strategy included a two-week commitment to begin—and

end—each day with the warmest smile I could offer Matt. At times this required me to pause and imagine what my face would look like if I was the newlywed—bright, cheery, a tiny bit bursting—and I did my best to replicate it. I'm not saying I always achieved it, but I did try.

Obviously the goal wasn't merely to plaster on a fake smile but to communicate my true pleasure in him, so this sometimes meant I would spend several minutes reflecting on those things about him that genuinely delighted me. These were usually small things: remembering his warm body next to me in the night, that witty thing he'd said to make me laugh, or a way in which he'd shown care for me or the kids. These were all simple pleasures that I could take for granted if I wasn't careful.

I didn't have to wait too long to see the results from this particular experiment. Not only did these morning smiles set a positive, happier tone for the day, but they set a sweeter one for the rest of our evening together too. The Experiment didn't solve everything that came our way, but no matter what else we would face, or had faced, in the day, I could cheer up, knowing, *Ah yes, but I'm so happy to have found you.*

Your Flirtation Experiment

Are you ready to share your delight of your husband directly with him? I can already anticipate an obvious question: "What if I don't exactly *feel* delight for my husband?" Right. At some point, poetry (and Hallmark movies) gets dropped into real life, and it's not as lovely as it first sounds. But here's the truth: delight is both a feeling *and* a choice. One easy place to start is the conscious decision to brightly smile when you see your husband, and let the feelings follow (even if it takes a while).

Although I focused on a loving smile for my experiment, there are other ways to show happiness for your husband. As you consider your own personality and relationship, what are some specific things you can do that would communicate your delight in him? The look on your face, the tone of your voice, the words that you say—they all add up to say (or not say), "I have found the one whom my soul loves."

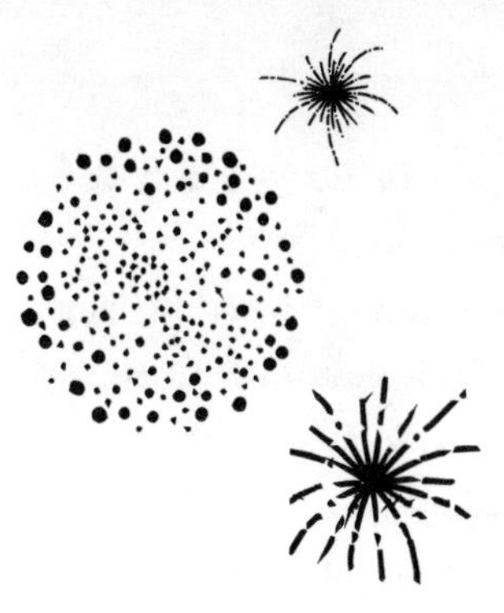

Chapter 17

Respect

PHYLICIA

Josh plopped a book on the coffee table and sighed.

"What's wrong?" I turned it over. It was a popular marriage book we were supposed to read for premarital counseling.

"It feels like it puts us in this rigid box." He ran a hand through his hair. "I mean, I want to be respected, but I want to be loved too."

I nodded—I'd felt the same way. During our engagement, we had learned that views about men desiring respect and women desiring love were not a full representation of our own relationship. I wanted to be respected, and he wanted affection and attentiveness.

A few days later I was listening to a sermon on marriage, and the pastor said something I'd never heard before: *Respecting your spouse requires showing respect in the way they best receive it. Not everyone receives respect the same way.*

Mind blown. I was familiar with love languages—ways of receiving and giving love—but this pastor suggested there was such a thing as a *respect language.* This made me curious: How did Josh understand and receive respect? I asked him.

"I think respect, to me, looks like paying attention when I'm talking even if you have better things to do," he said thoughtfully. "And maybe . . . being emotionally supportive. Being there for me. In many ways it looks a lot like love."

That conversation early in marriage has followed us through consecutive years. Josh's respect language doesn't match what I thought he would crave. I thought respect was almost like reverence or awe, that Josh would want me to commend him to other people, celebrate him publicly, and think highly of his work. In reality, those are things *I* value—not him. Josh feels respected when he feels loved. The more I evidence my love for him, the more he senses my respect.

At seven years in, I still struggle to respect Josh in the way he wants to receive respect. I get distracted or distant, and he begins to feel like he has little value in my eyes. He needs a clear reminder that he is seen and valued, that I both love *and* respect him.

This experiment was a simple activity not that much different from when I wrote him a letter and read it aloud (see chapter 13). It was a list: ten things I respected about him. Short, sweet, and to the point, my respect list differed in one way from my previous letter: my list was adaptable and repeatable. The ways we respect someone can change as they grow and seasons fade, so I see myself making more lists down the road. I sent the list via text (despite being home at the same time) and waited for him to read it.

Outdo One Another in Showing Honor

The Bible does not treat respect as a gendered virtue. From Exodus to Ephesians the Bible teaches women *and* men to show honor to other humans. Those "boring" laws in Leviticus? Most of them were protective in nature, guarding the value of human life—particularly the underprivileged—in societies that cared little about honoring the poor and oppressed.

How much more should we honor the image bearers with whom we have lifelong covenant? Anytime we see commands to the entire church, we should view commands specific to marriage *as part of* that greater mission—not in opposition to it. When Scripture tells us to love and honor other people, that means *all* people, including our spouses.

The Bible does not treat respect as a gendered virtue.

The Bible doesn't stop there. God could have commanded his people to be nice enough, but He is an extravagant and loving God, and His people are called to go above and beyond the worldly norm. This is why Paul said to the Roman church, "Let love be genuine. Abhor what is evil; hold fast to what is good. Love one another with brotherly affection. Outdo one another in showing honor" (Rom. 12:9–10).

Outdo one another. Make it your goal to do *more* for others than they do for you. Show them honor and respect even when you don't feel as honored or respected as you deserve. It's interesting also that Paul mentioned love twice and honor once; to love is to honor, and to honor is to love.

When we demonstrate love and respect, we give ourselves the freedom to walk in the commission Christ expects of His children. The apostle John admonished in his first letter, "Dear friends, let us love one another, for love comes from God. Everyone who loves has been born of God and knows God. Whoever does not love does not know God, because God is love" (1 John 4:7–8 NIV).

It does not say, "Let us love women" but "Love one another." Love your brother, sister, mother, father, female friend and male friend, husband or wife. Likewise, Paul added no caveat to Romans 12 when it comes to honor and respect.

The *Respect* Experiment

I texted my "respect list" to Josh while he was working downstairs and waited with bated breath to see how he'd respond. He usually replies quickly, so when he didn't say anything, I got a little antsy. Did he think my list was weird? Random? Did he not really care for it since he's not a words person? I got up from my chair and, out of the corner of my eye, spotted his phone charging in the corner. All that anxiety for nothing! He hadn't even seen my text.

He came upstairs for family movie night a few hours later. As we gathered in the living room with our snacks and hot chocolate, he looked up from his phone.

"Thank you."

"For what?" I feigned oblivion.

"For this list. It's really sweet."

If we weren't swamped with babies clambering for attention, I would have kissed him in confirmation.

To be honest, this experiment didn't feel super involved. I felt like it didn't make much of a difference. Wouldn't my words fade with time? If I'm to show my husband respect long term, what does that look like?

But as I read back through previous experiments, I realized *many of these reflect the loving respect I have for Josh.* Yes, they had different names. My actions wouldn't fit the marriage paradigm for respect that I grew up believing.

But biblical respect isn't just about appreciation or awe. Respect can be found in the trust that girds up laughter, in the risky step of vulnerability, in the heartfelt outpouring of admiration. It's speaking well of our spouses—which starts with *thinking* well of our spouses. Though lacking the respect terminology, many of the experiments before this one honored Josh all the same. And maybe that was the whole point: respect is a lifestyle of honor toward another human being. Josh's respect for me makes me feel safe and appreciated, and vice versa. And in respecting him—the person to whom I'm eternally bound—I learn a pattern of respect due to *all* people as image bearers of God.

Your Flirtation Experiment

What is your husband's respect language? What would speak loudest to him of your admiration? How could you show him honor as a fellow image bearer of Christ? Maybe your experiment will be simple like mine, or maybe you are more creative than I was.

Perhaps, like me, you have to dismantle a previous assumption about respect. Maybe the very word grinds your gears as you picture groveling and inequality. That's not what Scripture teaches about honor. Honor for others is the path of humility, which—in this wild, upside-down kingdom of God—leads to *our own exaltation* (Prov. 18:12).

You might have to ask your husband what respect looks like for him. That's what I did. Let his response inform your experiment, and you might be surprised by what you discover.

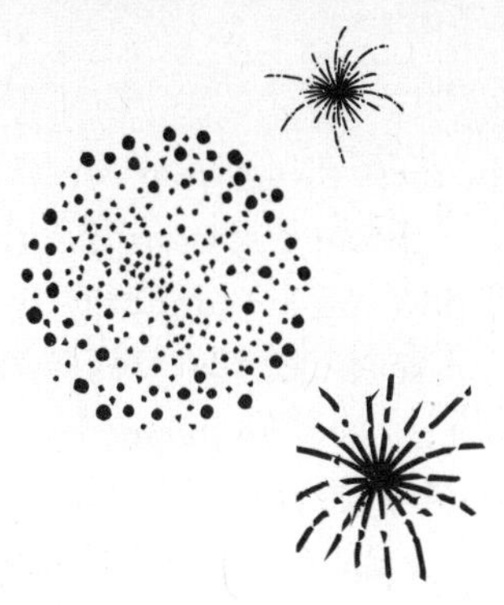

Chapter 18
Romance

LISA

As I was brainstorming for my next flirtation experiment, I playfully put the question to my hairdresser: "I'm working on this little experiment for my marriage and need some ideas for romance. Any suggestions?"

"Why not rent one of the honeymoon cabins up at the Five Pines?" she suggested.

I laughed at the thought. After nearly three decades of marriage and eight kids, Matt and I hardly qualify as honeymooners.

"Great suggestion!" I chuckled. And with the aluminum foil on my head glittering under the fluorescent lights, I began searching for those dreamy cabins on my phone—fireplace, blue-tiled soaking tub, convenient double shower!

We had been in a season of trudging, grinding, doing the next thing. I knew the furthest thing from Matt's mind was romance. Every marriage passes through seasons like this when connection and true, intimate fellowship are hindered. But that was okay this time because I was the scientist. This was *my* experiment. I made a conscious decision—a choice—to pursue Matt romantically. All he had to do was come along for the ride.

I'm not sure if it was the warm fire or the spa tub that drew me in, but suddenly I couldn't stop thinking about how lovely it sounded.

In no time, there they were on my phone, the Five Pines Resort "romance cabins," with a fantastic sale—two nights for the price of one! Before my hair was dry, I had booked a reservation for the following week. Two nights in a honeymoon cabin for two people who had been married for nearly thirty years.

I'd say the easy part was reserving the romance cabin. The bigger challenge was convincing Matt. Having grown up in BC, Canada, his idea of a cabin is more like a remote trapper's cabin many miles from anywhere or anyone. These local cabins, on the other hand, were neatly stacked in rows one right next to the other, with every luxury appointment (but to give them credit, you could view a wooded area from the back door). This kind of thing usually elicits from him a slightly raised eyebrow and a look of mild disdain. I knew he'd consider them *pretend* cabins—and maybe they were—but we could pretend for a couple of days, couldn't we?

The second hurdle was the timing. We were in the middle of a hectic and therefore stressful season. Time-wise we couldn't afford this mini-honeymoon adventure; it was an exceptionally inconvenient month to schedule a romantic getaway. (Is there ever a convenient time in our fast-paced twenty-first-century world?) Yet I managed to persuade Matt that this was precisely why we should do it.

And so off we went. After I grabbed our keys from the front desk, we crossed the small bridge to our little love shack in the woods, but it wasn't until we walked inside and closed the door behind us that it truly dawned on us: we had nowhere to go and no one to see for the following forty-eight hours.

Let the honeymoon begin!

God Loves a Good Romance

In the years from adolescence to womanhood, I don't think I ever put that pair of words together: *God* and *romance*. In my mind these were two entirely different topics, and one didn't have much to do with the other.

And yet I inexplicably desired romance—both before and after marriage. It didn't really make sense in my mind. Why would a fairly practical, down-to-earth Christian woman like me long for such impractical, intangible things?

Why? It's a question I mulled over for some time. Eventually I ventured to ask Matt what he thought this burning desire might be about.

Sure enough, my pastor husband had a ready answer. But he didn't turn to the Song of Solomon like I would have expected. Instead, he pointed right to the beginning of Genesis. "Look, the book starts with two naked people walking around in a garden, so desire is no surprise. Babe, think about it; it must've been beautiful and incredibly *hot*."

Interesting. I'd never thought of it quite like that but had focused on what came next instead. You know, the apple, the snake, the devastation of sin, and the banishment and murder that followed—that part of the story. That's where my mind immediately went.

And maybe that's where your mind goes too. But have you tried imagining what it must have been like before the fall? Lush and green.

Exotic and sweet. A man and a woman in their (ahem) natural state. Made for each other.

Eden must have been downright *steamy* in those beginning days—exactly how God designed it. Adam and Eve must have experienced some of the most romantic moments of all time. And you know what else I appreciate about this picture? How simple it all was. How very *natural*, how very *good.*

Eden must have been downright* steamy *in those beginning days—exactly how God designed it.

In light of creation and God's encouragement that man and woman enjoy each other—"Let her breasts satisfy you at all times; and always be enraptured with her love" (Prov. 5:19 NKJV)—it's not the least bit odd that we long for romance in our relationships. Don't be shy about stirring up the beauty and mystery of two people meant for each other.

The *Romance* Experiment

Although I originally hoped to make our romantic holiday a surprise, I ended up having to lay down all my cards to convince Matt to come along. Once we arrived, however, he entered into the spirit of it. He was the first to dramatically open the door to our small cabin while I was filming the grand moment with my phone. I was laughing the entire time . . . until I heard him click the door, playfully locking me out in the snow. *Very funny, Matt Jacobson!*

We hardly left the cabin for the next two days, except for the occasional run for food and fresh supplies. It was glorious. We had planned on making this something of a working vacation (part of the compromise of getting to go), but it turned out that, unlike the brochure promised, we didn't have reliable internet at our woodsy retreat. That was a source of frustration yet something of a godsend too.

So there wasn't much to do other than drink coffee, read our books, converse, *snuggle*, and soak in the sunken tub by the stone fireplace . . . and then snuggle some more.

In some ways, it really did remind me of the first few days of our honeymoon when we stayed in a cabin only ten minutes down the road from this current one—a coincidence I hadn't remembered when I initially booked the place.

I half teased Matt that we should go on a honeymoon like this every year.

"Good idea," he said and smiled in all seriousness.

Your Flirtation Experiment

Is romance not happening? Don't sit passively by and wait for it to magically appear. Take action. Pursue. You don't have to check into a honeymoon suite (or cabin) to enjoy a romantic holiday. Try brainstorming what might be marvelously restorative for the two of you. Think back to what you enjoyed together at the beginning of your relationship. Or consider something you've never done before, and try that.

Maybe for you, romance looks like camping in the wilderness or a festive evening out or attending a favorite event together—just the two of you.

And if you can't get away? After the kids are in bed, you could meet him on the back porch and watch the stars come out. Perhaps meet him in the bedroom with some coconut oil—great for back rubs!

Or you could set up an in-house picnic: spread a blanket on the floor, bring in a basket of goodies, and pour a glass of sweet something. Set aside a couple of hours to enjoy the God-given romance waiting for you.

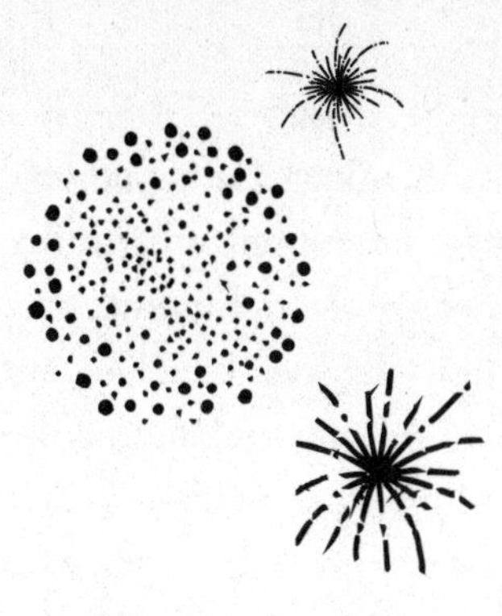

Chapter 19

Intimacy

PHYLICIA

Soon after we were married, Josh and I had a fight I'll never forget. It was in our newlywed apartment; I can still feel the brown laminate countertops under my hands and the freezing tile beneath my feet. The fight was the kind where you go in circles, never really getting anywhere. I was angry. Josh was bewildered. The angrier I got, the more I wanted to cry; the closer I got to crying, the angrier I became, until finally I shouted, "I just need to know I'm *enough*!"

I'd never expressed that to him—or to anyone, for that matter. I didn't even know I was afraid of being "not enough." This moment was pivotal. Though we continued to struggle in our marriage for a few more years, that moment marked the first time I made the connection between my anger and my fear.

Sometimes when we are afraid, we respond reactively, not

rationally. Until we can look at a situation objectively, our emotions will do the thinking for us. Among other things, anger can be a gut-level response to fear of loss, fear of intimacy, or fear of failure. In my case, I lashed out at Josh whenever I felt like I was failing. Anger is not a welcoming emotion, and my husband naturally pulled away from me. This made me feel more like a failure, which made me angrier—at myself, but manifested at him. What a crazy cycle!

Isn't this experiment about intimacy? Why are we talking about anger? I'm not a psychologist, but in my own life, anger and intimacy are connected—and according to *Psychology Today*, fear of intimacy can manifest as anger.[7] Anger was the only emotion I felt comfortable with. Other feelings, like affection or emotional intimacy, felt far too risky.

When Perfect Love Walks In

The apostle John described what God does to our fear when he said, "There is no fear in love, but perfect love casts out fear. For fear has to do with punishment, and whoever fears has not been perfected in love" (1 John 4:18). God is the epitome of love, perfect love. When you invite Him into the core of your being, into the darkest and most broken parts of you, He literally "casts out fear." He takes it by the collar and throws it in the street. Fear cannot live in the same space as the Spirit of God.

To experience the fullness of the Spirit's work, though, we may have to identify some root causes of our fear. Counseling and therapy are wonderful resources for this process. As I navigated my own aversion to closeness with Josh, one of the first places I looked was at the lies I adopted as truth. *How do these compare to the truth of who I am?* I asked myself.

Scripture has a lot to say about who we are in Christ. These truths are the measuring stick for anything else we believe about ourselves and our capacity for intimacy. Because of Christ, we are:

- newly created (2 Cor. 5:17)
- the workmanship of God (Eph. 2:10)
- no longer condemned (Rom. 8:1)
- children of God (John 1:12)
- the dwelling place of the Holy Spirit (1 Cor. 6:19)
- holy and beloved (Col. 3:12)

And that's just the beginning!

The lies start early. Many of them begin in childhood. Perhaps your lies came through abuse or neglect. Maybe they came from a perfectionist parent or the trauma of divorce. However the lies became part of your life, Christ enters in to take them out.

Because fear of intimacy is never just about intimacy, bringing Christ into this conversation early is vital. This fear is never just about affection or becoming emotionally bonded to our husbands. We can spot-treat our struggles, but unless we let Christ heal those inner wounds—and process them safely with wise people—our fear will resurface over and over again.

Perhaps you already know the truth of who you are in Christ. But do you truly *believe* it? It's not enough to know. We must allow that knowledge to become real for us, real for our wounds, real for the cacophony of lies. Until we believe we are enough through Christ, we will continue to second-guess our "enoughness" in marriage. Believing that God actually loves you, and that His love changes your life, is the first step to conquering fear. Fear can't be kicked out until Perfect Love walks in.

Until we believe we are enough through Christ, we will continue to second-guess our "enoughness" in marriage.

My struggle with intimacy was linked to how I dealt with my inmost fears. Because I was afraid of being vulnerable, I wouldn't accept the love of the person closest to me. The little steps of vulnerability, made through this experiment, helped me face my fear. And as I have let God into those fears (a continual process) and allowed Perfect Love to transform me from the inside out, I find myself capable of closeness.

The *Intimacy* Experiment

We often think of intimacy in terms of sex, but if you can't already tell, that's not the focus of this chapter. Emotional intimacy is the foundation for sexual intimacy. Emotionless sex may be physical and mental, but it lacks the bond of an invested heart.

For the first three or four years of marriage, I was perfectly happy with an emotionless, physical intimacy. It seemed like my best option. Paralyzed by fear, there was no way I would open up emotionally, especially in the bedroom. It took five years for me to say, "I love you," during or after Josh and I were physically intimate.

By the time I recognized my fears and began taking steps to heal them, my habits were well entrenched. The very idea of pursuing emotional connection with Josh intimidated me. I wanted to crawl back into my comfortable, impenetrable shell. At the same time, I knew we could only progress so far in our relationship if I refused to become vulnerable, if I remained at an emotional distance. So I experimented with saying, "I love you."

To some of you, this sounds basic. And I guess it is. But for those who struggle with vulnerability and intimacy, the simple act of initiating love (verbally or otherwise) is a step of courage. I already told Josh I loved him, but it was usually in response to him, not on my own accord. And I definitely didn't say it when I felt vulnerable. This was my season of change: I challenged myself to say it at least once a day and to say it at times when I really didn't want to.

At first the words lodged in my throat like the proverbial frog. I hemmed and hawed and tried to change my own subject. I didn't want to say it flippantly, and that's what made me nervous—I was saying it like I meant it (and I did!). What if he was caught off guard by the new, emotionally available me? In some ways, I felt like we were dating again: *Who's going to say it first?*

I remember the day that question was answered. We were sitting on a bridge in rural Virginia, our feet dangling over a pasture stream. A large black cow was peering at us through the barbed wire fence. Josh took my hand, and tears were in his eyes as he said it: "I love you."

I replied, "I love you too."

How could I forget? All the waiting that led to such a moment, the way time stopped, and I was delighted to hold his hand. How did seven years wear that down, grind it away?

The magic of that first "I love you" never has to go away. I get to keep it, and so do you.

Your Flirtation Experiment

Have you experienced the cycle of fear and anger? Your story might look a little different. Think for a moment about your temper. Do you struggle with anger? If so, ask yourself, *What am I afraid of losing when I get angry?*

Is it approval? Is it love? Is it control? Do you think if your husband ignores your attempt to hug him that you are losing his love, so you get afraid, but because you don't know how to express emotion, you get mad?

Get inside your own head today. This is going to take some time, so you might try setting a timer for ten minutes and really thinking about it. If intimacy (of any kind) is a struggle for you, let time, prayer, meditation, and counseling help identify the lies and causes that drive your struggle.

I don't want to minimize the journey to healing that I have gone through or that you may have to walk through to become confident in intimacy. But I do hope this encourages you: love and peace are still possible, no matter how unworthy you currently feel. Christ's love for us, and our acceptance of that love, helps us accept the love of our husbands. Being loved well and fully enables us to love others, no matter what lies color the past.

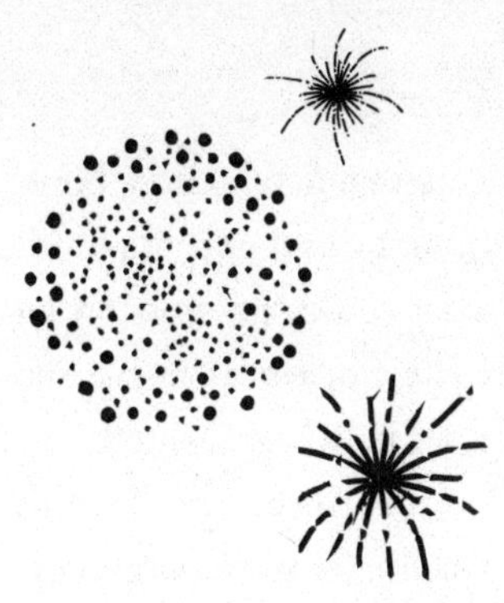

Chapter 20

Blessing

LISA

These days I seem to do my best thinking in the middle of the night. The house is quiet, and I have the space and time to let my thoughts run as they may without interruption. This particular night's theme was Matt's sixtieth birthday, which was fast approaching. And the dilemma before me revolved around what might be the perfect gift for the occasion.

Although I'd never describe my husband as "the man who has everything," choosing a present for him is still extraordinarily difficult. He'll deny it when he hears me say this, but you can trust my word: it's a challenge.

And now we had this significant event coming up—celebrating sixty years. Six decades of life. That seems noteworthy to me. I could never settle for a nice sweater or a new book. This gift should be meaningful and memorable, and nothing he could—or would—ever get for himself. But what could that possibly be?

The numbers on the clock next to me showed nearly 1:00 a.m. when I finally landed on it. *Words.* Matt loves words. So what better present than to bless him with the gift of words?

The following morning, I set to work contacting a wide variety of people who know and love my husband. I started with family, both immediate and some extended, and then went on to faithful, loving friends who have known and respected Matt for many years. Others were more recent friends but who "got" him from the get-go. The list was surprisingly eclectic—old and young, men and women, near and far—and its very breadth made my heart soar. So much like my husband, that list.

I made the list longer than I really needed, knowing that while many might agree to write something up, it was also likely that up to a third of the people wouldn't see it through. But I was wrong. Because every single person on the list wrote a word of blessing for Matt, I ended up with piles of kind notes and beautiful letters for him.

I soon realized that I'd want some way to organize all these carefully written words and quickly ordered an old-world wooden letter box to hold the treasures. I also found vintage stationery on which to print off each letter to make it look like it had been around for a hundred years or so. The plan was going perfectly.

And I excitedly counted the days until his big day!

Offering a Blessing

Blessings don't seem too popular anymore. The world may be moving on, but the power of blessing is not diminished. I have observed with my own eyes (and heart) the impact and lasting potency of a blessing spoken into the heart of another.

For me, it started with my children. The journey of motherhood had brought me to a place of desperation to communicate to our children my unmovable love for them and the positive future they had because of who they were in Christ. Uncertain of where to begin, I occasionally placed my hand on my children's heads when I'd walk by them, speaking a short word of blessing—of God's favor on their lives.

But it wouldn't work that way for Matt, as I doubt he'd appreciate my laying hands on his head. Nevertheless, I did want to speak words of blessing into his heart and mind.

Does the idea of offering a blessing sound strange or feel uncomfortable to you? I understand. But I can tell you firsthand there's something beautiful and enriching in marriage about offering a blessing to the man you love. Throughout the Bible we find many examples, like the man in Psalm 1:1–3:

> Blessed is the man
> Who walks not in the counsel of the ungodly,
> Nor stands in the path of sinners,
> Nor sits in the seat of the scornful;
> But his delight is in the law of the Lord,
> And in His law he meditates day and night.
> He shall be like a tree
> Planted by the rivers of water,
> That brings forth its fruit in its season,
> Whose leaf also shall not wither;
> And whatever he does shall prosper. (NKJV)

There's something beautiful and enriching in marriage about offering a blessing to the man you love.

Or something as simple as this: "I believe God's hand of favor is on you."

Words of blessing spoken over your husband show him clearly how your heart is inclined toward him and a positive future with him.

The *Blessing* Experiment

On the evening of Matt's birthday, I prepared a favorite dinner for our immediate family, and then we gathered in the living room around the fireplace to watch him open his presents. My gift was the last one, except that I snatched it from him before he could finish unwrapping it.

I wanted to give him each note, each letter, each blessing one at a time. One after another. And I called it right: he savored every syllable.

Our family sat there for well over an hour, looking on while he read each one silently to himself. He didn't share them out loud, just occasionally wiped the tears from his eyes and reached out his hand for the next one. We didn't mind; in some spiritual way, we were all taking part.

Admittedly this idea wasn't entirely new, as we have an informal tradition in our family to write a card or letter with our words of love and appreciation for the birthday person. What was special about it was that there were so many notes and they came from such a vast array of people who knew Matt in many different seasons of his life.

Sixty years of blessing stacked together in a single box.

Your Flirtation Experiment

Have you ever spoken words of blessing over your husband? Maybe this is unfamiliar territory for you, but it doesn't have to be formal or fancy. It can be as simple as speaking about who he is to you and about his future under God's favor. You can make your blessing an "occasion" by saying it in front of the entire family over dinner, or you can whisper it privately as he's drifting off to sleep: "You are a godly man. God's favor rests on you, and I am grateful to be your wife."

If this is a new concept and you're unsure what you'd say or are concerned that you'll get tongue-tied when you get ready to speak, try writing it out. There's nothing wrong with reading it from a note card or sending it to him in a text or leaving a handwritten note where he's sure to find it.

And if you're feeling as if the moment is right for your husband to hear a steady stream of blessing, consider asking other friends and family to join in. Just remember, more than anyone, he needs to hear it from you, the woman he married. And, as an experiment, you may be surprised to see the impact such an approach can have on the quality of your relationship as your husband hears, again, how positively and hopefully you think of him.

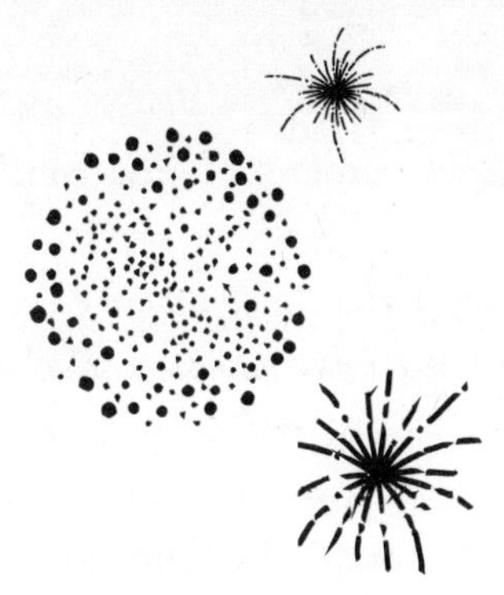

Chapter 21

Generosity

PHYLICIA

I'm a gifts girl. Christmas is one of my favorite holidays, and while I wish I could say it's all because of Jesus' birth, if I'm being truly honest . . . the gifts are up there too. But it's not just receiving gifts that lights up my heart; it's giving them! I love finding the perfect gift for someone I love—especially without a list. Surprise gifts? Yes, please!

Because of my love for gift giving, I tend to think of generosity in material terms. It wasn't until I was married (a few years in) that I realized generosity also applies to *time* and *attention*.

I had no problem giving gifts. I loved to spend money on Josh and my friends. But I was stingy with my time—so stingy, I became visibly annoyed at the smallest interruption. Worse, I was greedy with my attention. I spent hours on my computer, social media, or my favorite show, but if Josh wanted my full attention for ten minutes, I got bored and tuned out. This was a source of great conflict in the early years of our marriage.

You might be wondering, *If you were greedy with your time and attention, why didn't that come out in your dating season?* I've considered this myself. Because dating is periodic—meaning you're together for a time and then you go your separate ways—I was fully able to focus on Josh for our limited time together. Even in our first year of marriage, one or both of us traveled for work so often that we were separated a total of six months. It wasn't until we had our first child—when I quit my full-time job—that my problem with greed came to light.

"How was your day?" I'd ask when he finally came home after twelve hours in the field.

"Good," he'd reply. Then, as the minutes wore on as he filled in the details, I stopped listening.

I know—it's horrible. Listening has always been a struggle for me. I'm always looking for the next thing to get done, and listening just isn't efficient. If the story didn't involve me solving some problem, I wasn't interested.

Our Generous Jesus

Proverbs 11:24–25 has a profound word on generosity:

> One gives freely, yet grows all the richer;
> another withholds what he should give, and only
> suffers want.
> Whoever brings blessing will be enriched,
> and one who waters will himself be watered.

Giving is an exercise in trust. It requires faith that what is being poured out will be restored. It's fascinating that the author of Proverbs notes that those who withhold from others—whether with money, time, or attention—still don't have enough. They just want *more.* Greed is a never-ending cycle. You think you spent enough time on the phone, but it sucks you in again. You think you have enough money to spend, but you have to buy the next cute thing.

But those who bring blessing to others? They walk away rich. Perhaps not always materially, but definitely spiritually. They feel the impact of generosity in the peace of their souls, the joy of relationship, and the desire to give yet again.

Giving is an exercise in trust. It requires faith that what is being poured out will be restored.

When it comes to generosity of time, what better example do we have than Jesus? Jesus, with the most important ministry in the history of the world, frequently allowed Himself to be stopped, interrupted, and taken aside. Some of His greatest miracles were accomplished for those who called for Him, grabbed on to Him, and held Him back from where He was originally going (for example, Luke 7:11–17; 8:43–48; 17:11–19). Rather than become irritated at the delay, angered at the interruption, Jesus used the opportunity to give *even more* of Himself. Jesus gave His full attention to those who knew nothing of His majesty, and that love is our example.

The Generosity Experiment

My struggle to give my full attention—to anyone, not just Josh—has been ongoing since those early days of marriage. I knew that breaking such an ingrained habit would take work. To start, I had to discern what was pulling my attention away from Josh in the first place. Why did I get so irritated when I was interrupted? Why did I find fully focused conversations so hard? The answer was in the palm of my hand: my phone.

Yes, my phone. As a business owner, my phone is never more than a few feet away. When I find myself bored, I reach for it. When I want to check messages, find a recipe, look up the doctor's phone number, or send a quick text, it's always there. Like most of us, I spend way too much time with it.

At that time, it was almost like I was married to my phone, and it was getting in the way of my real-life relationship. I couldn't watch a movie without checking it. Because I was the one who struggled most, I never felt the sting of having a partner pull out their phone during one-on-one time. To me, it felt harmless. To Josh, it felt like being ignored. When he mentioned it, I got defensive and angry—after all, I was just trying to work. I deserved it; I was with the kids all day! Over time he got so discouraged that he stopped bringing it up and just went along with it. Soon our movie nights dissolved into two people mostly on their phones. My stalwart protection of time and attention gave me my space at the cost of our intimacy.

The phone was (and sometimes still is) the problem. To experiment with giving generously of my time and attention, the phone had to go. But it couldn't go completely, because I needed it for work. I decided to set up some phone boundaries to help me in the task. Every night from 6:00 to 9:00 p.m., I deleted my social media apps—completely. I didn't have the self-control to stay off of them, even with my notifications turned off. Deleting apps and shutting off my phone was the first step for me in learning to give generously to Josh.

It *is* true that you can have boundaries with technology and still fail to give your spouse full attention. With kids that's a daily challenge. But removing the phone from my equation took away the primary distraction from what matters most. Without my phone, the impulse to "check in" slowly faded, and I began to look forward to evenings away from my device. I especially came to love the day each week when my phone was off and away. It felt like breathing freely, like I could spend time with Josh without the pressure to respond, text, post, comment, or tweet.

And you know what's even better than breathing freely? Breathing freely with the one you love.

Your Flirtation Experiment

Do you, like me, struggle to give generously of your time or attention to your spouse? Maybe it's time: you struggle to sit still long enough to satisfy your husband's "quality time" love language. Or maybe you're great at the sitting part but you have to distract yourself with TV, a device, a book—you get the picture. Have you ever considered that time and attention can be a gift you give your spouse?

Of course, your spouse might not be great at giving these things back. In my own marriage, Josh and I both fell into a routine of hoarding time and refusing to be attentive. We let memes and supposedly urgent work tasks take over something special. But even though Josh was complicit, I couldn't make him change. I could only change myself, and that's where I started. I wanted to go back to the "I can't wait to be with you" feeling of our dating days. The best way to create that—I've found—is to stop hoarding my time and generously pour it out.

Where could *you* start? Do you have any boundaries for your phone use? When do you find yourself most drawn to using it? Think about the habits you have with technology and how that impacts your relationship. You don't have to be alone in this, either. I shared my phone boundaries with Josh and asked him to hold me accountable. This can be a team effort.

If you feel frustrated by this experiment, just remember: generosity, in anything, takes practice. It is a willful dying to ourselves, and that's not easy. Giving is a good work. It's a work that shapes and forms us into the image of Christ Himself.

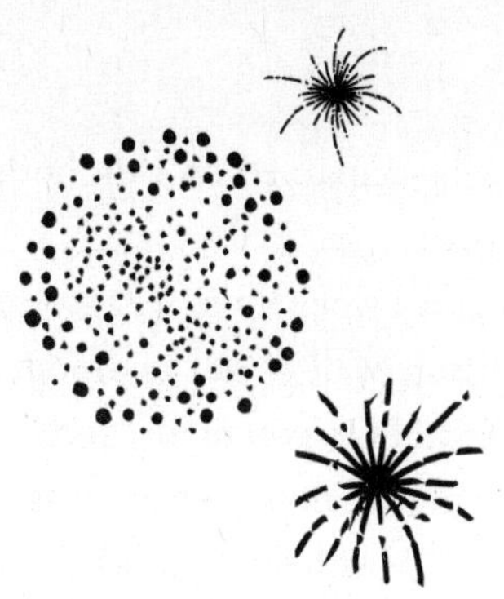

Chapter 22

Rest

LISA

The summer Matt's parents came to live with us, we had four children, five years of age and under. At the time, none of us knew it would become a long-term arrangement, and none of us knew what a journey it would turn out to be.

But about ten years into shared life with my in-laws, it became increasingly evident that Matt's mom had more than a little forgetful problem. No longer a matter of occasionally losing her keys or mixing up names, by then she couldn't remember her own husband's name ("that kind sir," she'd call him). As Alzheimer's continued its relentless destruction, her ability to recognize familiar faces faded years before the last stages of the disease took her home to be with Jesus Christ. And yet she always recognized her son Matt, the only one who could handle her increasingly impossible behavior.

So it was Matt who remained on call, both morning and night, during those many years.

One moonless night I woke up to what sounded like banging and scratching on the outside wall of our bedroom at 2:00 a.m. It was a cold, dark, windy Central Oregon night, and I couldn't identify what might be causing the strange noise, when I was startled to hear a voice desperately crying out, "Matthew, Matthew."

His mother.

We live on ten acres, surrounded on two sides by hundreds of acres of government (Bureau of Land Management) land. She often wandered from their home, adjacent to ours, in those days, and we'd resorted to many creative ways to keep tabs on her whereabouts, including locking the outside doors to their house at night. But she turned out to be a Houdini and somehow found a way to escape, again, that night.

Hearing clawing and thumping on the outside of your home in the wee hours of the night is disturbing. Alarmed, I shook Matt awake, and he ran out the front door to rescue her.

I lay there praying for a minute, trying to calm my spirit, then slipped out to the porch to see what went on with those two. Mom was standing in the yard, nearly naked, despite the cool night wind, frightened, bewildered, and alone. Then I watched as Matt gently wrapped his coat around her shivering, barely clothed body. Picking her up like a little child in his strong arms, he carried her across the lawn and up the steps to tuck her into bed. Past similar experiences told me he wouldn't return soon. After she finally drifted off to sleep, Matt found his way back and fell into our bed, exhausted.

When a couple exchanges marriage vows, despite the "for better, for worse" part, they don't anticipate such an eventuality. We had pictured scenarios of our promises—richer, poorer, sickness, and health—but carrying his lost, naked mother through the fall night back to her own bed was never one of them. Eventually life teaches you that married love doesn't always look like you think it will.

After ten years Matt's mom was taken into the loving arms of Jesus; but the year before she died, Matt's dad also went on hospice care. He remained next door in his home, and Matt became his primary caregiver as well—for the next five years. Then he, too, went to his rest, lying next to his wife of sixty-three years in the country cemetery.

Rest. We love them and miss them dearly, but there's the practical reality of it all too. After almost fifteen years of care, the concept of resting sounded like a dream.

Rest for the Weary

We can so easily underestimate our need for rest and how healing it is for our bodies. But rest is good not only for our physical selves; it is essential for our souls and for the souls of our marriages.

When we are overtired and overextended, exhaustion takes a toll on us, as well as on everyone around us, especially our husbands. It's not that we're weak. Nothing is wrong with us; we just were never meant to keep going on minimal sleep and constant demands.

But even if you can't enjoy eight hours of sleep a night (says this mother of eight children), you do have a source of rest you can always turn to—His name is Jesus. He openly invites us to come to Him: "Come to me, all who labor and are heavy laden, and I will give you rest. Take my yoke

Rest is good not only for our physical selves; it is essential for our souls and for the souls of our marriages.

upon you, and learn from me, for I am gentle and lowly in heart, and you will find rest for your souls. For my yoke is easy, and my burden is light" (Matt. 11:28–30).

Yet we tend to forget or ignore the heart of Jesus toward us and just keep marching on. Then we convince ourselves that we're the ones "paying the price" with our weariness; but we're not the only ones. If you're married to a man who "won't quit," then you know what I mean by that.

If you're a mom with young children, it's a given that you need rest. Or maybe you're a working mom or you're caring for aging parents or dealing with chronic illness. We have all kinds of reasons why we're desperate for rest.

While it's true there are some seasons when there's nothing much we can do other than to plow through, it's also true that we can tell ourselves that we have no choice when we actually do.

Is your close connection with your husband in jeopardy? Are you finding yourself overrun with priorities but losing the priority of each other?

Consider giving yourself—*giving your marriage*—the gift of rest.

The *Rest* Experiment

My husband needed sleep, but he also required rest—physical, emotional, and spiritual. I had known this for a while and felt somewhat helpless in what to do about it. By way of both personality and upbringing, he is resistant to resting. It's just not in his nature, even though he will acknowledge the concept.

Matt will insist that I sit down at the end of a long day. He'll be the first to encourage me to sleep in a little. He'll send me off for a break from all the busyness.

But he's not one to do that for himself. So, for this experiment, I gave him fair warning that I was going to get bossy with him. I wasn't sure what his response would be, but he only laughed. (Was he too tired to argue?) So, bossy I was.

Thankfully, our dear friends gave us an open invitation to visit them on their sweet farm nestled in the rolling hills of Virginia. It seemed the right time to take them up on their kind offer, so we headed out to spend a few quiet days in the country with them.

John and Susan were incredibly kind, spoiling us both with their generosity and thoughtfulness. We slept in late, drank lots of hot coffee, and devoured local fresh doughnuts. They took us for a hike in the country and stopped by an old generational orchard for crisp fall apples. The entire weekend we felt as though we were on the set of an old-fashioned film where we had surprisingly ended up being the stars.

And, best of all, Matt was able to rest, relax, and enjoy easy friendship and God's creation. That trip to the Virginia farm was better for us than twenty hours of therapy or any kind of exotic vacation you could name. It was God's gracious provision when we needed it most.

Your Flirtation Experiment

Rest doesn't sound very flirty, but the truth is, it's essential to finding our equilibrium and to pursuing and enjoying each other.

Who needs rest more: you or your husband? Likely both.

If it's you, then think hard about how you can get the rest you need—or, at any rate, more rest than you've been getting. Is it as simple as turning off the electronics and going to bed earlier? Making yourself lie down while your young ones take their naps? Cutting back on optional activities or commitments? Practicing the fine art of saying, "No, thank you. We're taking a season of rest"?

If it's your husband who could stand to slow down, that can be a tricky one. You might have to use your strong powers of persuasion to convince him. Maybe you could arrange for him to sleep in one morning and tell him you'll bring him breakfast in bed for a fun bonus. Or think through the many items on his plate and see if there's something you could (if only temporarily) take over to give him a break.

And if you both need rest, that will require extra planning and effort. If you have children in the home, you could consider asking family or trusted friends to watch them for a quick weekend getaway where you have nothing planned except sleep and relaxation. Or, if that sounds impossible right now, commit to an early bedtime for several nights in a row. You might be encouraged by what a few extra hours of sleep will do.

Making a commitment to rest is making each other a priority.

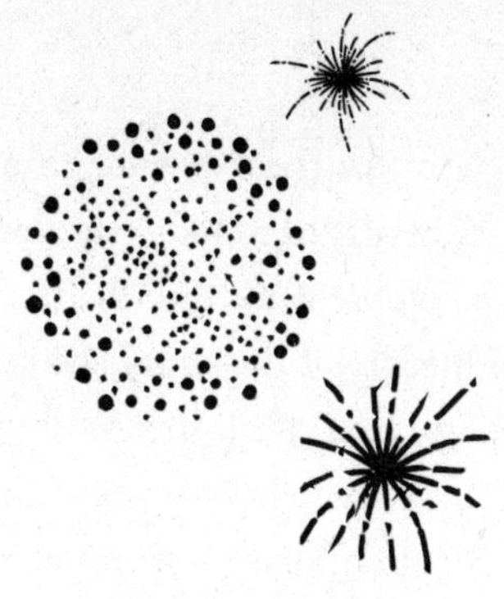

Chapter 23

Thoughtfulness

PHYLICIA

Almost two hours had passed since Josh had left to pick up the groceries, and I was getting nervous. Walmart was only fifteen minutes away. He hadn't texted back since I asked if he was okay. I finished feeding the baby and was about to call when I heard a tap on the living room's north window. My husband's hat and eyes were visible over the sill.

"Where have you—" I began, but stopped, mouth agape, as Josh lifted into view a twenty-pound . . . *salmon.*

His expression was like that of a little boy on Christmas morning. You could tell he was as pleased with my reaction as he was with the fish, but before I could ask any questions, he marched off to the garage with his catch.

While surprised at the timing of his catch (salmon was not on my list of groceries, but given that the river runs through our downtown, I can understand how he managed to snag one along the way), I was partially responsible for it. We were one month after the birth of our third child, in the midst of middle-of-the-night awakenings, lots of diapers, and my own postpartum healing. Josh was doing almost everything: cleaning, cooking meals, homeschooling our kindergartner, managing visitors, feeding our farm animals, and more. As a thank-you for all his work, I'd set aside some money for fishing supplies.

"The salmon rush is starting soon," I'd said one evening, handing off the baby. "And I want you to get whatever you need. You're postpartum, too, in a way."

He wasted no time. Once the gear arrived, it became a fixture in our minivan, stowed between baby car seats. The arrangement was comical to me, convenient for him—especially on grocery day.

I wasn't always this thoughtful though. In our season of small babies, I often felt entitled to the lion's share of attention. After all, I carried, birthed, and now had to recover from these babies. Josh's contribution to the whole process seemed—if we're being honest—rather small. But adding a child to the family (as with any life transition) affects both parties in a marriage. Josh might not have birthed our son, but he was bearing just as much difficulty in our season. A little thoughtfulness for his circumstances and interests didn't take much from me and brought him a lot of joy—and a lot of fish.

Our Husbands, Our Brothers

Scripture considers thoughtfulness a form of love. A perfect example of this connection is found in Philippians 2: "Do nothing from selfish ambition or conceit, but in humility count others more significant than yourselves. Let each of you look not only to his own interests, but also to the interests of others" (vv. 3–4).

Looking to the interests of others is an expression of love. Our consideration for the interests, burdens, and passions of our spouses reveals Christ in us. Something as simple as dropping Starbucks coffee off at the office, texting a prayer before a tough meeting, or—hardest of all—thinking about your husband's burdens when you're both in a stressful season shows thoughtfulness. And little actions like these can add up to living proof of our love.

Why is it so easy to show thoughtfulness to friends, extended family, or even our kids' teachers but not to our husbands? How many times have I bought a random gift for a friend who loves pugs, or sent a text to a friend before a big work event, or written a note to my daughter's Sunday school teacher but neglected to show such thoughtfulness in the home? I think this happens because we've forgotten the biblical mandate for "brotherly affection." Romans 12:10 says, "Love one another with brotherly affection. Outdo one another in showing honor." I tend not to see my husband as my brother. Perhaps it's a vestige of purity culture, where the guys you like are prospects and the guys you don't are "brothers in Christ." Perhaps it's my compartmentalizing husband and brother because I just don't think they belong in the same category.

But in the family of God, they do. Our husbands deserve our brotherly affection just like everyone else in the community of faith. This affection isn't so much about PDA as it is about a genuine appreciation for a person's character, and we can manifest this appreciation through thoughtful words, gifts, or service.

This kind of love is more than remembering birthdays and anniversaries. It's noticing our husbands' little contributions. Wives have a particular vantage point—a bird's-eye view—of their husbands' character. We will inevitably see their failures; it takes thoughtful love to emphasize their successes.

The *Thoughtfulness* Experiment

Thoughtfulness is one of my weakest points. Unfortunately, Josh came into our relationship believing otherwise. Before we were dating, Josh came down sick and—on my way home from an appointment—I picked up some DayQuil and dropped it off at his dorm. Josh thought this was incredibly kind and assumed this sort of behavior was my norm. Imagine his surprise when he discovered "the DayQuil incident" (as we came to call it) was a flash in the pan! Thinking of others' interests and needs does not come naturally to me. Thoughtfulness as a form of love is a seed planted by God, watered by the Word, and cultivated by taking action. The more I have tended to this area of weakness, the more fruit has grown. I am far more likely to think of Josh now when passing a Starbucks or driving past the river where the salmon run than I was seven years ago. Though I'm no fisherwoman, I wanted a gift that fit the amount of effort Josh had been exerting.

Loving him means thinking of what he loves.

I wanted to show him that I saw his work, I appreciated it and him, and I care about his passions—even if such passions delay the grocery pickup! And I chose to set aside the money for the fishing supplies as opposed to picking them out because I know how much Josh enjoys reading reviews—an added thoughtfulness for the man I know.

JOSH

Knowing that Phy was willing to invest in my hobbies had a profound effect on me. Her participation in a match of *Mario Party* on the GameCube showed she cared about my interests and happiness. She genuinely wanted me to find joy in an activity I could call my own. Her kind gesture spurred me to think about what would make her happy and how I could facilitate that. I brought that fish back like a cat leaves a bird on your doorstep. I was not only proud of my fine catch from the river but also proud of my fine catch of a wife.

Your Flirtation Experiment

Perhaps you don't have a river full of salmon in your downtown. Never fear! There are many ways to express thoughtfulness to your husband. You could do something simple, like dropping off a coffee at his work. But I encourage choosing something a little out of the norm, something that surprises him and makes him feel seen, known, and loved by you.

If you're like me, one of the harder areas to celebrate is my husband's hobbies. It can feel like hobbies are a distraction from the important things in the home, an inconvenience we don't want to encourage. Imagine how surprising it would be for your husband to know that you like when he has fun! Maybe you put together a snack basket for a video game night. Maybe you get him some gear for his next hunting season. Whatever it is, choose something specific and tell him exactly why you're giving it to him. Connecting thankfulness and thoughtfulness makes for a powerful gift.

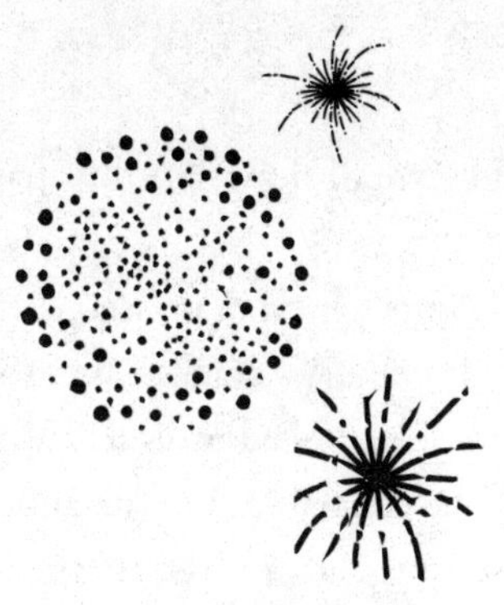

Chapter 24

Comfort

LISA

I found Matt sitting on the floor in the middle of a pile of papers, manila folders, and faded photographs. My husband had been next door for hours, and while I'd wanted to give him this time, I couldn't help worrying that he was over there alone and for so long.

Although Matt's dad passed away five months previous, his house—a small mobile home adjacent to our home on the property—had remained untouched. Everything was more or less just how we left it on the day he died.

And it was of increasing concern to me.

A few times, I'd softly suggested to Matt that we clean out his dad's place. Not that there was much left now, but among the remaining few pieces of furniture, there was a wonderful collection of family photos and a small drawer full of papers dating back five decades or so.

I feared I'd find Matt a little depressed sitting in his dad's room with so many years of memories stacked up around him. But, to my surprise, he smiled when he looked up and saw me standing over him. Almost immediately, he started telling me about an old picture he'd found of his dad hunting with our boys when they were still quite young—so little it's hard to imagine they could lift the rifle that was nearly the same size as they were. We laughed about that.

Matt had also come across a binder with his dad's reports from his years as a missionary bush pilot in northern British Columbia, each one carefully written out by hand. What trouble it must have been for him to write those out back then, yet what a blessing for us to have now. So much love, hardship, and history were crammed in that worn white binder.

Radically saved. Pioneer stock. Bush pilot. Gifted evangelist. That was Matt's dad. He couldn't meet a stranger without getting around to sharing the gospel.

In those final months, Matt had cared for his father day and night, doing what he could to make the last days of a man who had been slowly dying for a very long time as comfortable as possible.

And then the end was near. But what we thought would be the last hours turned into last days, even weeks. Matt's sister, Penny, came and helped as her work schedule would allow, but the lion's share of the care fell to Matt. By then he was approaching total exhaustion, so I insisted on taking the next shift.

In all honesty, I wasn't confident I could handle what might happen while over there, but neither did I want my husband walking through his dad's last days by himself. When Matt left that afternoon, I took Dad's sweet, rough hand in mine and quietly listened to his uneven breathing, nervously wondering if the next breath would be his last.

When Matt returned, he placed his hand over mine, and we tearfully said our goodbyes before I left the two of them together.

Giving Comfort

> Blessed be the God and Father of our Lord Jesus Christ, the Father of mercies and God of all comfort, *who comforts us in all our affliction*, so that we may be able to comfort those who are in any affliction, with the comfort with which we ourselves are comforted by God.
>
> —2 Corinthians 1:3–4

In all the years Dad lived with us, he wrote but one letter specifically to me. I still have it tucked in my Bible: three small papers written in his careful, shaky handwriting:

TO LISA, WITH LOVE
"GOD, HIS WORD TO YOU"
—COMFORT.

And below, he copied out over a dozen verses on God's comfort for His people.

Dad gave me that precious note when I was going through a particularly painful season of my own. He saw my distress, asked what was wrong, and the next thing I knew, I'd poured out the whole story to him. Although he didn't say much in the moment, the next time I stopped by, he passed those encouraging words to me.

I've read the verses he shared with me over and over again, wondering if he knew how deeply consoling they'd be. Here are but a few of them:

> Let your steadfast love comfort me
> according to your promise to your servant.
> —Psalm 119:76

> The Lord is near to the brokenhearted
> and saves the crushed in spirit.
> —Psalm 34:18

> "Blessed are those who mourn, for they shall be comforted."
> —Matthew 5:4

Perhaps you don't have a dear old, imperfect (but aren't we all?) saint such as my father-in-law in your life. But have you ever considered how beautifully and faithfully God comforts His people? How He desires to comfort you? He is the God of "all comfort," and He offers us His perfect comfort so that we, in turn, can comfort others. That's what His comfort of us is for—to share with others.

Maybe you're asking, *But what if we are both hurting? How can I comfort someone else when I'm aching so badly myself?* I hear you. Such a situation is very difficult to walk through together—and I say this out of personal experience—but please remember that the two of you are *one*. It's not "him" and "me"; there's only "us." Be sure your sadness is something that brings your hearts closer rather than pushes them farther apart.

Remember that the two of you are* one*. It's not "him" and "me"; there's only "us."

The Comfort Experiment

Matt is not inclined to share his grief with others. It's one of those things I've learned over our years together. He does cry, even weep on occasion, and he will certainly be there for anyone whose heart is wounded or in distress of any kind, entering into their sorrow and pain. But when it comes to his grief, he has a hard time letting anyone in—even me, his wife and closest friend.

Early on in our marriage, I thought the loving thing to do was to give him space. To let him work it out on his own since that appeared to be what he wanted—to be left alone. But I don't think that anymore. I am his wife, his soul mate, and I want to be a source of comfort to him.

This is relatively new territory for me because, for some unknown reason, I've never been a good comforter. Maybe it's my personality. Maybe it's my upbringing. But whatever it is, I feel incredibly awkward when someone is distressed or sad. My instinct is to cheer you up, pretend I didn't notice, or move on to more pleasant topics and feelings.

In other words, I might feel deeply for you, but you'd probably never guess it. So here I had two substantial barriers to cross in this situation: first his and then mine. As for the first, I had come to realize that I would need to take a risk and press in, even where it didn't seem wanted. Next, I had to overcome my uneasiness in this type of situation. Both felt like such huge hurdles to me.

Looking back, I realize how much I would have missed if I had played it safe and kept my distance rather than pushing through. Walking together through the grief of losing both parents held an unexpected sweetness in an otherwise sorrowful season in our lives.

Your Flirtation Experiment

Let's be reminded of what the Flirtation Experiment is all about. We're looking for closer heart connections and fellowship with our spouses. The Experiment is about how we meet our husbands where they are at, at various given times, for the purpose of entering in and building a deeper, more consistent, loving relationship. Can you relate to this chapter today? If not, there will come a time when you do, and you can keep it tucked away for that season.

Consider a situation where your husband needs comfort. Has he experienced loss? A death or disappointment? Write him a note of encouragement or gently recognize what he has been through. Tell him you care about his heart, or maybe don't say anything at all, and wrap your arms around him. Your quiet presence will let him know that you are with him in his sorrow.

We're instructed to "weep with those who weep" (Rom. 12:15), and sometimes the best thing we can do is silently sit in shared grief with the other person. He may communicate nothing, but don't underestimate his need for you to lovingly stay by his side.

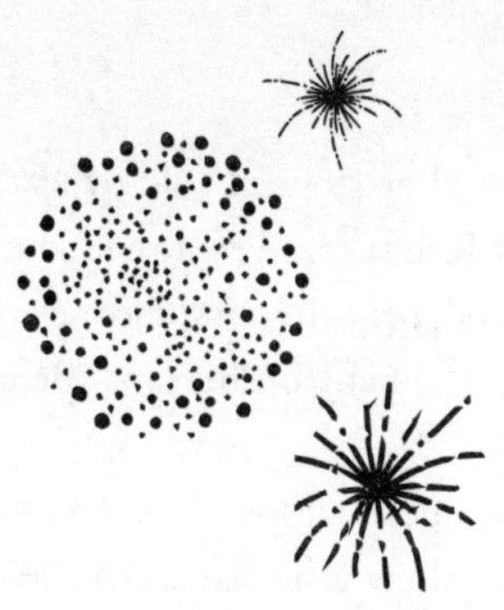

Chapter 25

Faith

PHYLICIA

I didn't tell Josh about the Flirtation Experiment until I came to the topic of faith.

Truth be told, I was stumped. *Faith. That's not a very flirty topic.* I could not figure out how to show Josh my faith in him—my belief in his character, his vision, his personhood—in a new and special way. Further, I wasn't sure I completely understood "believing in" a person at all. After a week of trial and error, I gave up and asked Josh bluntly at the dinner table.

"I am doing an experiment on you," I said, sliding the soy sauce to the side. "I was planning to show you how I have faith in you. Belief, I guess. But I don't know what that looks like. Like, what does it mean to have faith in a person? Or—I guess—you?"

Most people would be stopped cold by learning they'd become a glorified lab rat, but Josh breezed past that confession.

"I think . . . I think believing in someone is like being their cheerleader." He adjusted the baby on his lap. "Believing in what they've decided to do."

"Okay, but what does that look like practically? Like, how could I—or another wife—show a husband that belief? Or"—I grimaced slightly—"be a 'cheerleader'?" (Clearly, the Experiment was still not coming naturally.)

He replied, "I mean, it's different for every marriage. But for me, it's things like 'That workout looks really hard; good job!' or noticing when I have followed through on something." He stopped to think, then gave an intriguing distinction. "It means a lot when you thank me for things. For instance, 'Thanks for doing your quiet time with the Lord,' but the difference between this and thankfulness is that faith recognizes something *I* decided to do of my own accord. Thankfulness feels more like recognizing something you wanted me to do. Which is fine; it's still meaningful. But it's different."

I left the conversation, mulling over Josh's perspective. Never in a million years would I have perceived "thank you" as potentially guilt inducing (which isn't what he was saying but could be inferred). I was in a predicament: because I'd asked Josh directly what constituted faith in him, he would know what I was doing when I tried it out. This made me hesitate—but why?

The reason: I didn't want to be told what to do, then do it. I thought my actions would have less meaning since I didn't think of them myself. I fell for the age-old marital lie that says displays of love must be completely spontaneous. It's the lie that says we must implicitly know what our spouse desires—without asking them, without seeking specifics, and without being told their inmost needs. I'd been handed a blueprint for how Josh liked to be loved, but I didn't want to follow it because it wasn't *special.*

Love Believes

Tucked into the famous love passage in 1 Corinthians 13 is an attribute of love we often miss. We blow past it, carried by "Love is patient and kind" to "Love never ends" without pause. But there, between bearing burdens and stalwart hope, is a love that "believes." Other translations say love "always trusts" (e.g., NIV). I think we can safely gather that love gives the benefit of the doubt to those it reaches.

One of the hardest practices in marriage is this extension of trust. Believing in the goodwill of our spouses requires an incredible amount of forgiveness and self-awareness. After all, these are the same spouses whose words and actions hurt us at times. We can only extend belief if we understand the power of grace and are aware of our own failings.

It is from this belief in the good intent of our husbands that we build toward belief *in* our husbands: truly supporting and encouraging who they are. I can't believe in someone who I am convinced has ill intent. But I can throw all my loyalty behind a person who—though flawed—is doing the best he can.

> ***Believing in the goodwill of our spouses requires an incredible amount of forgiveness and self-awareness. After all, these are the same spouses whose words and actions hurt us at times.***

I'll be the first to say that this isn't easy. My job requires filtering a lot of information through a critical lens, measuring what is true, right, and good against false, wrong, and evil. I struggle to exchange that critical eye for a believing spirit. But when I do, cheering my husband on in the goodness of who he is creates a "bond of peace" in our marriage (Eph. 4:3).

The *Faith* Experiment

I swallowed my pride and used Josh's insight. Who knows better what constitutes belief than the person you're believing in? I did, however, wait a day before saying anything; it would have been too obvious.

The following day, we completed our afternoon workout together. I had noticed that he was more in shape since starting a particular program, but I honestly felt awkward saying anything (why do I still do this?!). If I did, wouldn't it seem like I was playing a part?

I mustered courage against the awkwardness and told him I was impressed by his gym progress. But—figuring specifics would be more helpful—I told him *how* it impressed me. "I know being consistent is hard, but I can tell you've been doing it."

Over the next few days I tried to capture that cheerleader essence in what I affirmed. What did he choose to do? How could I support that? The first day it was his workout; the next day it was his parenting; later it was how he handled our finances. I asked myself, *If I were single, what about this man would impress me?* I thought back to those early days of dating; what would make me call my sister, tittering about how great this guy was? Those were the things I chose to speak into. By the third or fourth time, it didn't matter that Josh had told me how to have faith in him. What mattered was that I believed it. I believed in him.

Through this exercise I realized that the fear of being fake is the biggest roadblock to being genuine. We can't get to authentic compliments and faith in another person if we stay hung up on how we're perceived. And I don't know about you, but I've never questioned the authenticity of a compliment from someone who loves me. I gave Josh the benefit of the doubt: he would believe my words to be genuine. And guess what? He did.

Your Flirtation Experiment

Are you hung up on displaying love because you fear being fake? Do you think only spontaneous expressions count? If you do, you might not love your husband as effectively as you intend. Most of us are fine with a love language test guiding our actions but not with asking our spouses to tell us what means the most to them—and then actually doing it!

Or maybe you struggle to give your spouse the benefit of the doubt, to risk trust. I won't suggest that this experiment (or the others) will fix that overnight. Marriage counseling is always a good idea for processing through those barriers. But even in a healthy marriage, believing in a spouse's goodwill is helpful to communication.

What is something your husband does that you could affirm? What is something you can celebrate and cheer on? Focus on that! Celebrate it!

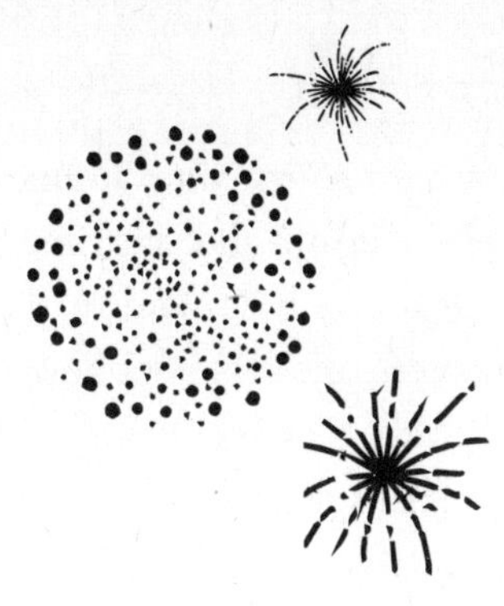

Chapter 26

Tenderness

LISA

I never thought I'd have a country music song to thank for helping my marriage.

It started one night when we were snuggled in bed, sleepily watching a show, when Matt suddenly and inexplicably turned it off. The next thing I knew, he had switched over to YouTube, and we were listening to a heart-wrenching song about a daughter's love for her father to whom life and people had been very unkind and who "could use a little mercy now." It took me a second to place it, but then I recognized the song as one that had been playing in the background of the closing scene of that episode we were viewing earlier.

But it wasn't the music video I was watching; I was studying Matt. It was evident from the abrupt break and the pained expression on his face that something about that song deeply resonated with him. And I wanted to understand what it was and why.

As I'd been distracted the first time around, when the song was over, I asked if he'd play it again, and this time I closed my eyes and listened carefully, both to the lyrics and to the singer's voice. The words were simple enough—mostly about how every one of us needs mercy—but somehow that message, along with her gentle sound, made a surprisingly powerful combination—so powerful that it could tug at a grown man's heart.

After that evening's experience I concluded that something was missing—or at least lacking from other people—in my husband's life. That much I could see. As I searched for the word that would describe what that thing might be, it came to me at last: *tenderness.*

That country song had brought something of a revelation, and in some ways, our marriage will never be the same because of it.

Searching for Tenderness

Although the exact word *tenderness* isn't in the Bible, there is a word that expresses the idea beautifully. It's the Greek word *eusplagchnos*, often translated into English as "tenderhearted"—a layered word that also includes compassion and even pity—and it's found in two places in the New Testament: "Be kind to one another, *tenderhearted*, forgiving one another, as God in Christ forgave you" (Eph. 4:32), and then in 1 Peter: "Finally, all of you, have unity of mind, sympathy, brotherly love, *a tender heart*, and a humble mind" (3:8).

Perhaps you're already familiar with these "tender" verses and just haven't yet thought about them in the context of marriage. I suspect that's the case for many of us. We're too inclined, consciously or unconsciously, to dismiss these (and other) biblical admonitions when it comes to our husbands. But when Scripture gives instructions to "one another" and "all of you," it doesn't exclude your marriage relationship; on the contrary, it's a good place to begin.

Perhaps you've only been unaware (as in my case), but it's also possible you have your reasons for not expressing more tenderness in your marriage. Maybe you're struggling with resentment, or softening your heart toward your husband feels too vulnerable. Or perhaps it has nothing to do with him directly but goes back to wounds or disappointments inflicted by others in the past.

If we could talk over a cup of tea, I'd look into your eyes and tell you I am truly sorry for what you've been through, and then I would lean in and touch your hand and softly, gently, lovingly remind you that hardening your heart is never spiritually or physically healthy. And it's never a long-term solution. Doing so may feel protective or safer to you in the moment, but it will prevent, and eventually completely destroy, the rich marriage relationship God wants for you. When you choose tough over tender, not only is your husband sadly missing out, but you are too.

When you choose tough over tender, not only is your husband sadly missing out, but you are too.

The Tenderness Experiment

Although I don't think Matt would ever describe me as being hard-hearted, I was nevertheless moved after that night to contemplate how I might demonstrate more tenderness toward him.

Here are the simple steps I purposed to take. I found that same song we'd listened to together and put it on a playlist on my phone. Then I committed to listening to it every day for a month (yes, I'm serious). I wanted to capture that poignant moment and make it a permanent part of my heart.

Next, I considered the physical aspect of tenderness. Matt and I are already the touchy type, but that doesn't mean he couldn't use more hugs or a gentle caress—not in the sexual or even affectionate category, but the kind of sympathetic touch that says, "I care."

Lastly, and for me, this was the most significant change: I wanted to speak with a gentler voice. Now, I'm not a harsh person, far from it; I'm just more matter-of-fact. On top of that, I'm efficiency focused and I'm often in a hurry, so I can come off as short or clipped. I've discovered that being tenderhearted takes time. I wanted to slow down as well as soften my voice.

What would this look like on any given day? Besides listening to our song, I tried watching for when Matt might be hurting or feeling heavy. I married a man who can carry a lot, so I haven't always caught on to when he could use a tender touch or word. But I'm trying to be more sensitive and aware now.

Then when I did sense there was something troubling or weighing on him, I'd ask, "Are you okay, honey? Is there anything I can do?" But I didn't just throw those questions out there while I was busy picking up the living room or answering an email. I made a point to stop what I was doing, connect with his eyes, and listen carefully to his answer. Even if I can't fix or change anything, I can offer him my tenderness—my heart—and follow up with a soft touch.

Your Flirtation Experiment

Before starting this experiment, take some time to consider your own heart. Would you describe it as tough or tender? What would your husband say? And if you do struggle with tenderness, why is that? Are you holding on to a grudge? Are you ready to let it go? Aren't you glad God doesn't hold a grudge against you? Or maybe it's a deeper issue, pressed down somewhere in your heart, and it's time to work through it with your husband, a trusted friend, or Christian counselor. Selfless tenderness brings a sharing touch to marriage.

Consider your way of being. What are some of the specific ways you can express more heartfelt, genuine tenderness toward your husband? Don't make it more difficult than it needs to be! Sometimes it's the simplest gesture that communicates compassion: a warm hug, an understanding word, a concerned voice, and a caring countenance. Pick at least one of these, and then watch for that moment when your man could use a little tenderness from you.

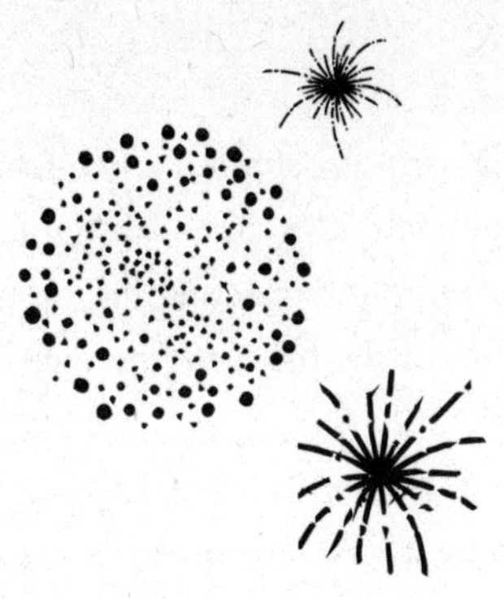

Chapter 27

Covenant

PHYLICIA

Earning a trip to Hawaii wasn't on my radar—until it happened. Through my work, Josh and I were able to attend an all-inclusive trip to Kona right before our sixth anniversary. To say we were thrilled is an understatement! Leaving the frigid tundra of Michigan for seventy degrees and a black sand beach sounded like nothing short of a dream.

This wasn't our first trip alone together since kids came along, but it was our first since we started marriage counseling. The previous fall we had noticed that our communication wasn't what it should be. Constant misunderstandings (usually over the same things) plagued our interaction. Trust was hit or miss, and although we both knew that we loved each other, we often wondered if we *liked* each other at all.

Counseling was a welcome step for us. Through the weekly meetings, we learned to see each other in a new light, to be sympathetic to differences, to set better boundaries on phones, to express our feelings to each other regardless of the risk. In short, we learned to tend to our covenant.

So this trip was a celebration: a celebration of our growth as a couple, the covenant we kept—or rather, the covenant that kept us.

Halfway through the trip I was contacted on social media by an online acquaintance. "My friend is a wedding and travel photographer in Hawaii," she said. "She wants to gift you a photo shoot. Can you make it work?" I coordinated some details, then asked Josh if he'd enjoy the surprise. "It could be really special," I suggested. He agreed, if for no other reason than to have some nice pictures.

As a blogger, I've experienced plenty of photo shoots. But when we received the questionnaire for this one, there was something . . . different. The questions required us to share not how we met or when we married or why we were there, but what we admired about each other. What we noticed. We answered the questions individually, without seeing each other's answers. A few days later, on the last day of our time in Kona, we bumped down a lava road in a black Jeep to meet our photographer, Gabby.

Gabby and her husband had a story very similar to ours. They were opposites in almost every way, and the first years of their marriage were incredibly hard. Trust and healing came at a high cost as they mended hurts that ran deep. As Gabby shared her story, tears filled my own eyes—because she was also telling ours. She was telling a story of a covenant kept.

She walked us to the black sand beach and asked us to live out some of the answers from the questionnaire.

"Phylicia, run your hands over Josh's arms—you said you found those most attractive about him." Josh laughed, and I did too. While walking to sit on the shore, waves splashing our feet, Gabby turned to Josh. "Josh, tell Phylicia something you love about her. Look her in the eyes to say it."

As the session progressed, she encouraged even deeper, more intimate actions: "Phylicia, pray over Josh for a moment, and thank God for what you have together." We stood beneath the palm trees, damp from the warm water, with black pebbles all over our feet and salt water in our hair. I held his hands and prayed over him, over us.

Even though a camera was clicking the entire time, the moment was incredibly vulnerable, emotional, and unforgettable. I could see that Josh felt like I did—that this photo shoot on the beach, led by a couple who knew the hard beauty of keeping a covenant—would become a marker in our marriage.

More Than a Promise

We don't use the word *covenant* much, even in weddings themselves. It's an old term with definitions so antiquated that people forget what it means. Marriage is a covenant between two people—but it's a reflection of a much greater covenant, one between God and man.

God uses covenants in the Bible to bind Himself to people with promises. In His covenant with Abraham, God walked Himself "down the aisle" to fulfill both sides of the vow (Genesis 15). In other words, He took on the full responsibility to fulfill His covenant to Abraham. A covenant was an unbreakable promise, a binding agreement.

From the very beginning of marriage—the wedding day—our culture downplays covenant. We can write vows that possess little substance. We can walk out of the vow if it gets inconvenient or if we fall out of love. But that is not how covenant operates in the kingdom of God. Here, covenant is truly "for better or for worse . . . till death do us part." Just like Jesus and the church (Eph. 5:31–32).

To keep a covenant is not just to avoid infidelity but also to keep free from contempt. It means fighting for the vow that was made—not fighting *with* each other but fighting *for* each other. To battle on your knees and in your heart for the union an entire world wishes to bring down. Keeping a covenant looks a lot like war.

Peace cannot exist without protection. It must be guarded; it must be armed, because enemies of peace don't care about keeping it. The Enemy of marriage doesn't care about keeping your covenant. He wants anything but peace and unity between you and your husband.

So we go to war against contempt, against disunity, against anger and bitterness and anything that sets itself up against the union that God Himself brought together. *We keep the covenant.*

The *Covenant* Experiment

Setting up that photo shoot wasn't a turning point in our relationship. Rather, it was the culmination of years of hard work in our marriage. It was an hour of remembrance for everything we fought to build. It was a way to honor who we have become as a couple and to celebrate the covenant we have kept.

When you have spent a long time just keeping your head above water, doing crisis management or attempting to communicate through the same issue *again*, marriage feels like nothing more than a drawn-out argument with intermittent date nights. And in making progress—in choosing to honor each other, in making counsel a priority—we can become "box checkers" who miss the very point of the progress we're making: intimacy. Scheduling the photo shoot pressed Pause on it all. We took the time to celebrate our marriage, moments captured on camera to be framed on a wall.

I would be lying if I said I was completely comfortable throughout the shoot. Sharing vulnerable thoughts and emotions in front of someone I barely knew? No, thank you! But Gabby made the shoot a great experience. And even if she had not been as great as she was, the practice of voicing my thanks and admiration, even in front of others, was a powerful act I won't soon forget.

To watch Josh's eyes grow misty when I told him what I admired most, and to hear his voice say the same, can't be measured or contained. Even the photos of those moments can hardly capture the power of them. We left the shoot visibly impacted and were quiet on our way back to town.

"It really was special," Josh said. And it was.

Remembering covenant involves some looking back:

Each argument we ended with "I still love you."
Each day we forgave the weakness of the other.
Each moment we chose to reject the bitter thought.
Each time we sought counsel and godly wisdom.
Each time we obeyed the counsel we received.

And as the memories play through our minds, we can remind ourselves that we're not alone in this lifelong commitment. In keeping the covenant, in seeking God's will for our marriage to stay strong and unified, *the covenant kept us*. Christ keeps His own.

JOSH

It had been almost six years since our wedding—the last time I had shared something so intimate with Phy in front of an audience. Though you can hardly call our photographer an audience, being vulnerable and professing my love to Phy before a witness was powerful. It's easy for me to say "I love you" before we go to bed at night or in a blog post or in a book. But saying those words to each other with someone else there to hold me accountable and to capture that moment forever was an impactful experience for me. All the arguments and disdainful looks we endured from each other the past fall were all washed away with the black sand that day on the beach as Phy looked up into my eyes with no shield held up, no barricade standing, with eyes as tender and weak as gates wide open, letting me into her soul. We shared something unforgettable and have beautiful pictures as reminders of the covenant we made together—the decision to truly love each other.

Your Flirtation Experiment

Like Josh and me, you might consider setting up a photo shoot—not for an anniversary or family photos—simply to celebrate *you* as a couple! If your photographer doesn't have a questionnaire like ours did, you can write up a few questions and share your answers during the shoot.

If photos would make you or your husband uncomfortable, or they are out of budget, consider writing out your favorite memories of your marriage, the hardest moments you're now grateful for, and things you admire or find attractive about your husband. Set up a date and read him your answers.

Another way you could honor keeping your covenant is to have a vow renewal or a dinner party with your closest friends to celebrate how far you've come. Perhaps you could schedule a "just-because" adventure, and when your husband asks why, tell him it's for this—for keeping a vow.

What is a creative way you can celebrate the covenant you've kept?

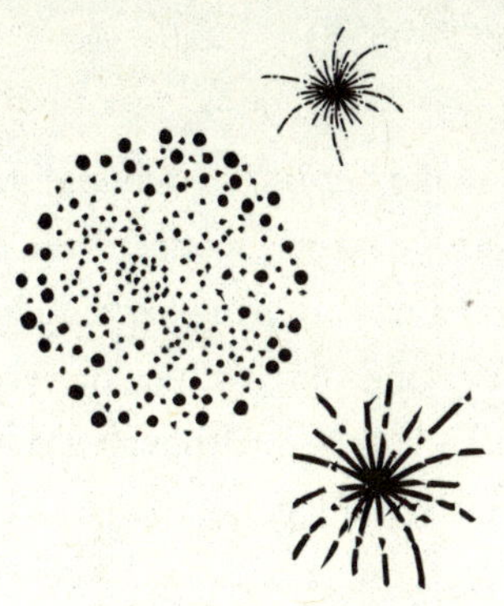

Chapter 28

Hope

LISA

Hope is our fifth child's middle name.

She was born with a severe medical condition, and her life was touch-and-go for those first few heartrending years. Following my emergency C-section, the doctors were painfully straightforward with us: "We're very sorry, but your daughter will never walk, talk, or even know you as her parents . . . if she makes it at all."

That was such an unexpected and devastating prognosis for our tiny baby girl. And what could we do but pray, and, in faith, slip Hope into the middle of Avonléa's name?

From the beginning, her daddy committed to be this little girl's champion. As soon as we brought her home, after months in the NICU, he plopped her down in the middle of the dinner table to join the rest of the family—tubes, cords, medical equipment, and all—determined to make her life as rich and meaningful as possible. It didn't matter where we went (a concert, the lake, the beach, or the mountains), he found a way to bring her, and her wheelchair, along.

Twenty years later and our Avonléa has exceeded every expectation any doctor ever had for her. Although she has limited use of both her legs and left arm, she manages quite well with her one strong right arm. One of our Jacobson maxims is "There's always a way to get something done!" and Avonléa embodies that truth every day. It's true that she remains childlike, but then she'll say something so insightful or recount some fact gleaned from a conversation four years previous that it amazes us all!

This dear girl has a gift for making us laugh (and occasionally weep), but she is always, *always* a joy.

As soon as I received an invitation to the Country Dance, I hoped our family would attend—and secretly planned to make it part of my flirtation experiment. After all, who wouldn't want to dance the night away in a lush green field? Waltz out under the stars?

Apparently not everyone. Avonléa squealed at the prospect, but our three teenage sons had a slightly less than enthusiastic response: "Ah, Mom, do we *have* to go?" "*Why* are we doing this?" and other similar protests. Judging by the look on my husband's face, he wasn't entirely keen on the prospect either.

But I thought the evening sounded simply magical.

The God of Hope

In the early days and months of our daughter's life, no one offered much hope for Avonléa's life—or for our marriage either, for that matter.

I learned this one day while roaming the hospital halls. The head

NICU pediatrician pulled me aside and felt compelled to pass on these sobering statistics: "I thought you should know that 85 percent of couples who give birth to a severe special needs child like yours end in divorce."

Oh . . . thanks. Our baby hadn't completed her second brain surgery, and there we were, discussing the statistical probability for our divorce.

The doctor's stark statement filled my head with many anxious thoughts and questions as Matt and I waited together in the hall. *Would the challenges of this fragile baby tear us apart? The sleepless nights, the hospital stays, the financial strain, the grief—would they be too heavy for us to carry?* I wondered, and I deeply worried.

But then my mind went back to the name God had graciously given us for her—that promising Hope—and tearfully considered how much greater He is than any medical or social statistics. And I poured out my heart to Him in that moment—and the many moments following. You could see the numerous places where my Bible is marked up, highlighted, and cried over:

> My hope is in You.
>
> —Psalm 39:7 NKJV

> Hope in the Lord;
> For with the Lord there is mercy,
> And with Him is abundant redemption.
>
> —Psalm 130:7 NKJV

> May the God of hope fill you with all joy and peace in believing, that you may abound in hope by the power of the Holy Spirit.
>
> —Romans 15:13 NKJV

And you? Are you clinging to hope? I don't know the details of your life or your particular circumstances, my friend, but I do know this: you can trust God with your heart and, yes, with your marriage. Our God is able—more than able—to bring beauty to your situation, whatever that may be and no matter how hopeless it may currently seem (see Isa. 61:3; Eph. 3:20).

Remember, the Flirtation Experiment is all about being a biblical woman and wife; you have so much to contribute to the upward direction of your marriage. So take courage and take action steps without apology or reserve.

We also know that God's Word tells us that whatever we do, we are to do it "as to the Lord" (Col. 3:23 NKJV). When you have that perspective, you don't have to base your feelings on what did—or didn't—happen in response to your efforts. It's in God's hands now.

Our God is able—more than able—to bring beauty to your situation, whatever that may be and no matter how hopeless it may currently seem.

Naturally, as women with hearts and feelings, we desire our efforts returned to us, *with interest*. That's only normal. But, truly, if you choose to have as your motivation pleasing your heavenly Father, then you can freely pour love into your marriage and trust God for the rest.

The *Hope* Experiment

When we arrived at the dance, the trees were brightly strung with rows of lights, and more rows of lights outlined the dance floor, the rugged Cascade Mountains serving as a stunning backdrop to the entire scene. Many of the dancers had come in full costume—women in long, sweeping dresses and men in dress shirts, ties, and vests. And families were everywhere, mingling, eating, laughing, and, of course, dancing.

Matt and I spotted a warm seat near the firepit and waited with Avonléa while our boys went in search of dance partners. We didn't speak to them again for the next two hours—so much for the reluctant dancers! We tapped our feet as they danced the Virginia Reel, the Fairfield Fancy, Chasing the Fox . . .

And then, finally, the waltz.

Up until then I'd been content to observe the line dances, but my real intention was to snag a slow dance with Matt once the waltz music began.

But just as I started to stand, we both looked over to see Avonléa in her wheelchair, happily clapping her right hand against her little, curled left hand. We exchanged glances and, without a word, both knew what would happen next. Matt walked over and slowly rolled her wheelchair across the bumpy grass into the middle of the field and gallantly asked, "May I have this dance?"

She gave a little girl's giggle, and then he swept her up, holding her tight—her legs dangling down, two feet off the ground—and twirled her around under the night sky.

Although the dance turned out differently than what I first envisioned, clearly that night was meant for our sweet girl to shine instead.

And as I watched those two together, I reflected on those early traumatic weeks, months, and years when we had no idea we'd end up here like this—that there would be laughter, joy, and even dancing. For some reason, that doctor didn't think to mention that our daughter might bring so much delight or that caring for a severe special needs child can also pull people closer together rather than splitting them in two.

Or that God might have beautiful plans for us that defy any grim prognosis or depressing statistics.

Your Flirtation Experiment

If you're looking to fold hope into your own flirtation experiment, here are a few starter ideas to consider: arrange for a special dance night. Put together a playlist of your favorite love songs and invite a few friends over. Or if you prefer something more private, try playing *your song* after dinner some evening and ask your husband to dance. No need to make it overly formal—it's a chance to celebrate the two of you!

Have you been listening to discouraging voices either in the past or currently spoken around you? Have you believed their dire predictions that "your marriage won't make it" or "you'll end in divorce just like the rest of the family," or something similar? If so, recognize that this is not from the Lord. He can do *all things* and is not held back by sad statistics, destructive family patterns, or past experiences. Remember: we serve the God of all hope!

Look up as many verses as you can find in the Bible about hope. You might be surprised, and definitely encouraged, when you see how many there are. Pick out a few favorites, write them out on pretty paper, and place them in strategic places around your home and claim them as your own.

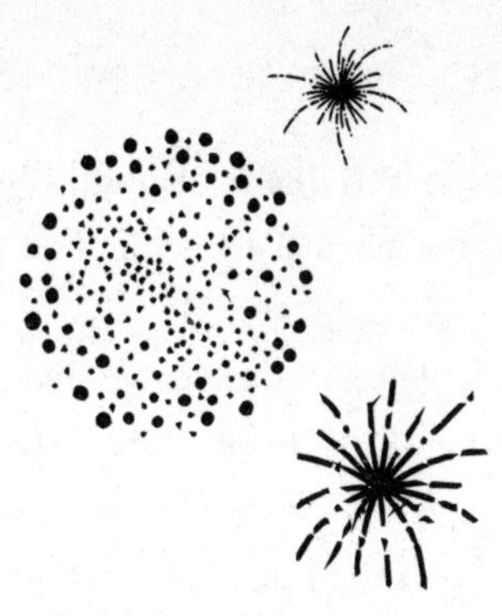

Chapter 29

Healing

PHYLICIA

Before I opened my eyes, I smiled: *January 2*, my favorite day of the year. I swung my feet out of bed. To say that I was excited was an understatement. I love everything about the new year: the sense of newness, a fresh beginning, going after goals. It was 2016, I was finally coming out of postpartum with our first baby, and life felt normal. Our little duplex was still decorated for Christmas as I trotted downstairs to answer some emails.

I didn't know that I would be devastated a few hours later. I didn't know how deeply I would be hurt by my husband, or how, in a desperate attempt for direction, I would go for a run and find myself sobbing in a public park, the fog of my breath fading with my plans.

I won't get into the details of what happened; they aren't necessary now. But if you've ever been deeply hurt by your spouse, you know what it feels like. It feels like the floor falling away beneath you. It feels like a sting and a twist. It feels like being utterly, completely alone.

I've felt that kind of hurt a few times in my marriage. I felt it once during the writing of this book. My husband is imperfect, and so am I. Both of us have deeply wounded each other, wounds that have slowly healed to scars—but even scars twinge sometimes. In marriage, "forgive and forget" is often impossible. I flip a page in a photo album and my stomach drops; that old pain rises. Is healing possible?

In 2019 I learned that physical healing takes a lot longer than expected. A freak accident in a soccer game broke my left leg in two places. I was scheduled for surgery right before the Fourth of July and spent the entire summer on a couch or in a wheelchair. I didn't walk freely until October; didn't run until November of the following year. Even now, walking upstairs can send a painful reminder that my leg was broken. The scar still hurts. The plate and screws can still be felt. I'm healed, but I'm still healing.

Like bodies, hearts take time to heal. And time itself can't heal all wounds; it just fades them. We see a face or a name, flip a page or hear a song, and the pain is right there all over again, as strong as it ever was. Betrayal isn't easy to overcome. Hurt doesn't disappear just because you ignore it.

But old wounds *can* heal. I am proof of that.

I'm not suggesting that healing is all up to the wife. Husbands must own their mistakes. And it takes good counsel and prayer, effort and humility, to make progress in a marriage marred by hurt.

I'm in a marriage committed to the long term—for better or for worse—and in those "for worse" moments, we've had to do some hard work of healing. I can't control that process for Josh, but I can pursue it—and him—for myself.

Peace to Those Far and Near

Every marriage to a good man is also marriage to a sinful one. None of us brings perfection to the marriage covenant. Perhaps that's one reason the Bible uses marriage as a picture of Jesus' relationship to the church. He is the perfect bridegroom with an imperfect bride; we can never deserve Him, yet His love restores us again and again. His wounds bring us healing, and His reconciliation brings us peace.

The person most deeply wounded by the sins of our husbands is not us but God. It grieves God to see His people hurt. It grieves Him to see His people hurt others. In Mark 3:1–5 we see Jesus grieved and angry by the hardened hearts of the Pharisees. Their lack of compassion and refusal to care for the least of these would have kept a wounded man from healing. They were concerned with doing what was right *in their eyes*, but not with the restoration of a fellow human. This account deals with physical healing, but threads of its truth are woven into the wounds of marriage. Have I, with hardened heart, wounded my husband? And have I let my wounds harden my heart toward him?

The answer is yes to both. But for healing to occur between spouses, healing must start between Christ and me:

> He was wounded for our transgressions,
> He was bruised for our iniquities;

> The chastisement for our peace was upon Him,
> And by His stripes we are healed.
>
> —Isaiah 53:5 NKJV

Jesus was wounded for every hurt I've inflicted. But He was also wounded for every hurt inflicted upon *me*. My husband's hurtful behaviors and actions have seemed insurmountable at times, but the forgiveness of Christ enables me to forgive others—including the person closest to me.

> "I have seen their ways, but I will heal them;
> I will guide them and restore comfort to Israel's mourners,
> creating praise on their lips.
> Peace, peace, to those far and near,"
> says the Lord. "And I will heal them."
>
> —Isaiah 57:18–19 NIV

The Lord offers healing and peace to the most undeserving. Sometimes I need to remember just how much I'm forgiven before holding a measuring stick against Josh. If my husband repents, do I give him the chance to heal our broken bond? And if not, who am I to refuse my husband the very thing offered to me through Christ? Clearly, I am not talking about situations of abuse and recurrent manipulation. In a healthy marriage, our husbands will hurt and offend us—sometimes deeply. And those wounds will take time to heal. But for healing to happen, I've had to open the door to reconciliation, something I can do only if I experience the reconciliation of Christ.

My marriage has had some incredibly difficult, lonely years.

There were years when I lay in bed at night, staring at the wall, wondering if I made the wrong choice—and Josh, with his back to me, lay wondering the same. We stayed because of our covenant. We stayed because of the hope of healing: "Heal me, Lord, and I will be healed; save me and I will be saved, for you are the one I praise" (Jer. 17:14 NIV).

I can't work peace in my marriage with my own sinful hands. But I know Someone who can: Someone with hands scarred by wounds received in innocence. Someone who has seen my ways *and* my husband's and offers to heal us both. Jesus offers peace to my marriage. Jesus takes those who are far and brings them near.

The Healing Experiment

In truth, this entire book could be called *The Healing Experiment*. I started these "flirtations" to add fun to my marriage. But what I didn't say in the introduction is how much hurt my marriage has endured. The Flirtation Experiment was meant to be fun, but it is also a balm to the scars of our early days.

There is no fast track to trust building. Josh and I would have a great week followed by a comment the next that brought back all the memories of contempt and disdain, of coldness and distance. In a flash, four years of progress would disappear. We were enemies once again, glaring steely-eyed over our coffee cups, passing silently through the rhythms of our day.

I couldn't bear to go backward. Josh didn't want to either. So I began these experiments to keep in touch with my love for him, to find that flirty, sassy girl he dated long ago. I wasn't sure that writing letters and telling jokes could make a difference (hence the name "experiment"), yet each day I pursued Josh was a step into restoration. Each pun I told, each word I wrote, each kiss in the kitchen dealt a blow to the problems of our past. In seemingly insignificant ways, I fought for healing. And healing is what God brought.

Your Flirtation Experiment

I hope the experiments you've done thus far have been as healing for you as mine have been for me. This chapter's experiment, in truth, is to continue doing what you've done before: to keep pursuing, to keep investing in your marriage, and, most of all, to keep inviting Christ to be your center. Perhaps you're in the middle of some deep hurts, hurts that require counseling and outside help—don't wait to seek that out. Counseling has been essential to healing for Josh and me. But when the counseling appointment is over, we have to walk out what we've learned. That's where I become responsible for my own forgiveness and where I begin the daily work of seeking God and seeking Josh.

Don't be discouraged if healing takes time. That's the nature of it. Just starting the Flirtation Experiment is a step in a restoring direction.

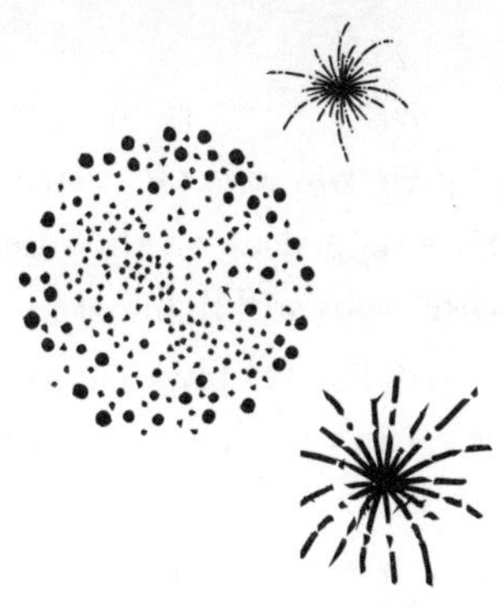

Chapter 30

Joy

LISA

Sometimes it's hard to imagine that life will ever change. As a couple, you can get so wrapped up in the days that you're hardly aware of the years. Then suddenly there you both are, and life is no longer how it's always been.

I suppose Matt and I should have seen that day coming, but due to all the normal noise and needs around us—kids, parents, work, ministry, a busy world—it rather snuck up on us.

But one day not too long ago it hit me that we had arrived at a new season in our marriage. There we were, sitting together in our living room chairs early in the morning as we had done thousands of times before—virtually every morning since the beginning of us—sharing a pot of French press coffee. Except, on this particular day, somehow, things felt strangely different.

On that morning, it was only us. Two lovers sipping coffee together and talking, wrapped up in the interwoven details of our lives. Our younger three sons still living at home were either at work or in class. Even our Avonléa was preoccupied with her own project. So, after all this time raising all those kids, we were returning to the two of us.

Years had passed. Life was making massive changes right before our eyes, and we had hardly noticed.

Suddenly aware of the sea change, I turned to my husband of all those years and began bombarding him with a cascade of unexpected concern and frantic emotions. *Did he see the momentous changes coming our way? Did he realize we'd soon be considered empty nesters (except for our Avonléa)? Were we really ready for this next season?*

He listened quietly, as he tends to take such things in stride. Always has. He didn't see the big deal and only smiled at the prospect, but for me, this realization rocked my world. Or at least gave me a whole lot to think about.

Down to him and me. Growing old together. Not that I've dreaded our empty-nester season, even commenting often over the years about how much I'm looking forward to sharing that season together. But in the moment, all of a sudden, wow!

Choosing Joy

Our world is absorbed with the elusive search for happiness, and yet what we truly wish for is something far deeper, far more satisfying than "happy"; we long for *joy*.

For the believer, joy is one of the strong characteristics of genuine

Our world is absorbed with the elusive search for happiness, and yet what we truly wish for is something far deeper, far more satisfying than "happy"; we long for **joy.**

Christian faith—a fruit of the Spirit (Gal. 5:22). It's what we experience in God's presence. Psalm 16:11 declares, "You will show me the path of life; in Your presence is fullness of joy; at Your right hand are pleasures forevermore" (NKJV). And Jesus comforts us with His words, saying, "These things I have spoken to you, that my joy may be in you, and that your joy may be full" (John 15:11).

But you'll also come across joy in some strange and unexpected ways in Scripture, such as, "Count it all joy, my brothers, when you meet trials of various kinds" (James 1:2). We're called to choose joy when life brings changes—even difficult trials—that we would never choose for ourselves. When I was a young woman, I found this verse to be rather disheartening (if not downright impossible), but the older I've grown, the more I see it as an encouraging one—recognizing that our sense of peace and contentment, the joy we choose to walk in, doesn't have to depend on the people, places, or circumstances around us.

Even in the changes that life brings, including those hard and heartbreaking trials, we can, in faith, choose joy—a settled confidence that God is with us, has a beautiful future in store for us, and works all things together for good to those who love Him (Rom. 8:28).

Whatever else might be swirling around us, as Christians we can truthfully say, "It is well with my soul." We are, in fact, encouraged to do so. And no one or nothing can take the joy of the Lord from us. When you draw near to the Father (James 4:8), wherever you are in life, you are never out of His hand.

Something must have shaken me up to come up with a plan like the Sunrise Experiment. Because, honestly, it's so out of character for me that you'd just have to suspect *something* was off.

Matt certainly did.

"You want us to leave *when*?" He could hardly believe what he was hearing.

I tried to sound matter-of-fact. "We need to be ready to leave the house no later than 6:00 a.m. tomorrow." I said it as if this kind of thing happened all the time. While I knew he'd be taken aback by my required departure time, I hadn't expected him to be quite so utterly shocked.

"You're telling me that *you* are voluntarily planning an event that involves waking up while it's still dark and in below-freezing temperatures? During a holiday weekend when you don't have to get up? Leaving the house without a shower?" The man was genuinely astounded (which probably tells you more about me than it does about him).

"Exactly!" I said with clipped certainty. He looked at me from his chair, over his glasses. "This is very unusual, but I'll be ready."

The birds on my alarm started chirping at 5:45 a.m. Matt was already up. (Of course!) The cozy covers were holding me back, but I eased out of them and slipped on my jeans, heavy winter coat, and knitted wool hat. I didn't tell him where we were going, but there are only so many options at that hour and time of year in Central Oregon, so he had guessed it had something to do with the sunrise.

And he was right. After picking up an Americano for him and a latte for me, we drove out to Smith Rock State Park with its dramatic cliffs, world-renowned for rock climbing. But locals also know that it happens to be a gorgeous spot to catch the sunrise—if you're up early enough to get out there, that is.

We had no trouble finding a parking place at that hour or in that weather (eighteen chilly degrees!). We grabbed our coffees and walked out to the viewing area where we could watch the sun come up, shining in all its magnificent glory across those famous jagged cliffs to the south and the more than three-hundred-foot vertical flat face directly behind us.

When the sun broke over the eastern horizon and forced away the predawn shadows, reflecting its glory off of the face of Smith Rock, I could feel what the psalmist must have meant by "joy comes in the morning" (Ps. 30:5 NKJV).

As we sat silently together, enjoying the transfiguration of the night to day, Matt's strong arm pulled me closer, and he said while looking at the rock, "Thank you, babe. God is good."

MATT

Lisa never ceases to surprise me. That whole morning was so out of character; I was incredulous. *Really? We're doing this?* It was awesome and so much fun! But it was also so much more than that. Somehow our surprise sunrise date turned my thoughts to the deeper things of our love for each other and the coming glory to be revealed when Jesus Christ returns. So it really turned out to be all about love—our love for each other and God's love for us.

Your Flirtation Experiment

Perhaps it's been a while since you've considered what kinds of experiences or activities move your husband past happiness to deep-seated joy. Has time passed since you both had a moment to reflect on the presence and goodness of God in your lives and reminded yourselves that He is there, in control and offering His best for you and your marriage?

Maybe you and your husband can catch a sunrise together as we did, or perhaps settle in for a beautiful sunset. In preparation, sit down and write out the many things—no matter how small—you have to be thankful for, even with the difficulties you may be facing today. On your special joy experiment, you might share with him your list of things you are thankful for. How much our husbands appreciate a grateful spirit in their wives!

You also might make your list together as a beautiful way to see how truly good God has been, giving confidence for a future that might be looming with seeming uncertainty. "Seeming" uncertainty because you serve a God who loves you and with whom nothing is uncertain—the very foundation of security and joy.

Closing Note

Our dear friends,

We feel we can call you that now that we've shared so much together. How are you feeling about these experiments? Are you seeing a new horizon of hope for a richer, more passionate and connected marriage as you take action and pursue your husband?

We are genuinely excited for you to embark on your own Flirtation Experiment. We've profoundly enjoyed sharing our personal lives with you, but our greatest wish is that you will boldly take the next step in your own pursuit.

Of course, you may want to try some of the flirtation experiments we did—you can hardly go wrong with bringing in more kissing or building him up with your words—but don't stop there. You and your husband are unique with your own personalities, desires, and individual dynamics, so let your imagination go and create experiments that expressly fit you.

One thing you'll want to keep in mind is that this isn't an instant pot for making deep, beautiful marriage relationships. Yes, everything we share here really did take place, and it actually did make a difference, but these things developed *over time*, not overnight. Don't be easily discouraged or tempted to believe that nothing is happening when you've only just begun. *Perseverance* is a good word to keep in mind.

Start small and watch for little sparks, especially at first. That's how blazing fires are ignited!

We'd also like to gently remind you that it doesn't help to compare your relationship (or your husband) to ours. Let us assure you that we're not special: we've spilled our tears, experienced hurts and disappointments, and been stretched in the most unexpected ways as we walked through the experiments shared in these pages. Life happens to us all.

And yet.

And yet we can also honestly say these flirtations have brought about significant changes, even transformation, to our marriages. God has powerfully used our Flirtation Experiment to turn everyday situations into true romance and brought us a closer heart connection. We can't wait to see what He has in store for you and yours!

In His grace,
Lisa & Phylicia

Notes

1. Nina Terrero, "Romance by the Numbers," *Entertainment Weekly*, October 17, 2014, https://ew.com/article/2014/10/17/romance-numbers/.
2. C. S. Lewis, "Charity," *The Four Loves* (New York: HarperCollins,2017), 155–56.
3. Gretchen Rubin, "Act the Way You Want To Feel," (blog), November 6, 2009, https://gretchenrubin.com/2009/11/act-the-way-you-want-to-feel/.
4. R. William Betcher, quoted in Kira M. Newman, "What Playfulness Can Do for Your Relationship," Greater Good Magazine, February 11, 2020, https://greatergood.berkeley.edu/article/item/what_playfulness_can_do_for_your_relationship.
5. Lewis, "Charity," *The Four Loves*, 155.
6. C. S. Lewis, "Friendship," *The Four Loves* (New York: Houghton Mifflin Harcourt, 1991), 65.
7. Leon F. Seltzer, "Anger and Intimacy: Incompatible but Unavoidable Housemates," *Psychology Today*, June 12, 2019, https://www.psychologytoday.com/us/blog/evolution-the-self/201906/anger-and-intimacy-incompatible-unavoidable-housemates.

About the Authors

LISA JACOBSON is an author, a podcaster, and the founder of Club31Women.com, an online community of Christian women authors who write on marriage, home, family, and faith—a powerful voice for biblical womanhood. She is the author of the bestselling *100 Ways to Love Your Husband*. Lisa and her husband, Matt, are also cohosts of the popular *Faithful Life* podcast. They live in the beautiful Pacific Northwest where they have enjoyed raising their eight children.

PHYLICIA MASONHEIMER is a national bestselling author, speaker, and host of the *Verity* podcast. Her blog, *Every Woman a Theologian*, teaches Christians how to know what they believe and live it boldly. Theology touches every area of life, so Phylicia addresses cultural questions through the lens of church history and sound biblical interpretation. She lives in northern Michigan with her husband and three children.

Connect with

Lisa and *Club31Women!*

Club31Women.com

Cohost of the *FAITHFUL LIFE* Podcast

Follow along @Club31Women

CONNECT WITH PHYLICIA AND EVERY WOMAN A THEOLOGIAN

PHYLICIAMASONHEIMER.COM

AUTHOR / HOST OF VERITY PODCAST

FOLLOW ALONG @PHYLICIAMASONHEIMER

TEACHING CHRISTIANS HOW TO KNOW
WHAT THEY BELIEVE & LIVE IT BOLDLY.
PHYLICIAMASONHEIMER.COM